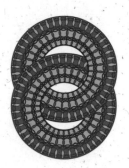

THE BREATH OF PARTED LIPS

# THE BREATH OF PARTED LIPS

## VOICES FROM THE ROBERT FROST PLACE

---

### VOLUME ONE

Foreword by
**Donald Hall**

CavanKerry ❧ Press LTD.

FORT LEE, NEW JERSEY

For complete acknowledgments of copyright holders
and publication rights, see page 381.

Library of Congress Cataloging-in-Publication Data

The breath of parted lips : voices from the Robert Frost Place.
p.     cm.
ISBN 0-9678856-2-0
1. American poetry—20th century.  2. American poetry—New Hampshire—Franconia.
I. Robert Frost Place (Franconia, NH.)
PS615.B647 2001
811'.5408—dc21          00-47379

Cover photograph of Robert Frost by Ken Heyman, courtesy
Dartmouth College Library Special Collections

Cover and text design by Charles Casey Martin

FIRST EDITION

*For the people of Franconia*
*Whose woods these are*

# CONTENTS

# FOREWORD

## DONALD HALL

W hen Robert Frost was introduced as a farmer poet, he stuck out his hands, palms up: These aren't a farmer's hands, he would say. Famously, he declared that once a man had made a metaphor, it unfitted him for other work.

Frost had his chosen work, and we are thankful for it. He consecrated his whole life to the art of poetry.

When I met him, in August of 1945, he was seventy-one years old and I was sixteen. The first moment I saw him he was walking uphill toward an assembly room at Bread Loaf, and he seemed to rise from the ground like a stone figure. He was not stone, but he endured with the firmness of granite, obdurate in devotion to the art he loved. When I saw him in the last August of his life, he was deaf as granite, but spoke with his old skill, humor, and intensity. The books he was reading then rested beside his chair: Horace's Odes, and a new edition of Robinson's Chaucer.

He was not always an easy man. He was often an uneasy man, whatever fame and praise accrued to him. He cherished and defended his place among poets, and like Milton and Keats his ambition was boundless: He wanted above all to make poems that would last.

Unlike most of us, and many of the greatest poets, he mostly worked alone. If Frost worked little *with* other poets, he worked for poets and poetry. In 1957, in an introduction to an anthology of new poets, he wrote: "Young poetry is the breath of parted lips. For spirit to survive, the mouth must find how to firm and not to harden." To firm and not to harden. In Franconia's Frost Place, young poets learn to firm their mouths without hardening their hearts.

From its beginning in 1977, The Frost Place has celebrated the ongoingness of American poetry. Every year, a younger poet spends the summer in Robert Frost's old house overlooking the glorious valley and the mountains beyond. The poet has a modest stipend, leisure, and the opportunity to work where Frost worked. Every year, the summer's resident and other visiting poets read their poems aloud—summer performances of contemporary art among the White Mountains. Visitors may walk where Frost walked and inspect the rooms where he lived with his family and wrote poems.

The Frost Place in Franconia is a monument to a great American poet. We need our monuments. We honor poetry as we honor the poet where the poet lived. Frost and his family resided in this Franconia house beginning in 1915 after they returned from England. Great poems were written in this house.

Poetry flourished at the Frost Place then and it flourishes there now.

*—Donald Hall*
*Eagle Pond Farm, New Hampshire*

# THE
# FIRST RESIDENT

◆

Poems selected by
# Donald Hall
from
*Mountain Interval*
1913–1915

# ROBERT FROST

## The Road Not Taken

Two roads diverged in a yellow wood,
And sorry I could not travel both
And be one traveler, long I stood
And looked down one as far as I could
To where it bent in the undergrowth;

Then took the other, as just as fair,
And having perhaps the better claim,
Because it was grassy and wanted wear;
Though as for that the passing there
Had worn them really about the same,

And both that morning equally lay
In leaves no step had trodden black.
Oh, I kept the first for another day!
Yet knowing how way leads on to way,
I doubted if I should ever come back.

I shall be telling this with a sigh
Somewhere ages and ages hence:
Two roads diverged in a wood, and I—
I took the one less traveled by,
And that has made all the difference.

# An Old Man's Winter Night

All out-of-doors looked darkly in at him
Through the thin frost, almost in separate stars,
That gathers on the pane in empty rooms.
What kept his eyes from giving back the gaze
Was the lamp tilted near them in his hand.
What kept him from remembering what it was
That brought him to that creaking room was age.
He stood with barrels round him—at a loss.
And having scared the cellar under him
In clomping here, he scared it once again
In clomping off;—and scared the outer night,
Which has its sounds, familiar, like the roar
Of trees and crack of branches, common things,
But nothing so like beating on a box.
A light he was to no one but himself
Where now he sat, concerned with he knew what,
A quiet light, and then not even that.
He consigned to the moon, such as she was,
So late-arising, to the broken moon
As better than the sun in any case
For such a charge, his snow upon the roof,
His icicles along the wall to keep;
And slept. The log that shifted with a jolt
Once in the stove, disturbed him and he shifted,
And eased his heavy breathing, but still slept.
One aged man—one man—can't keep a house,
A farm, a countryside, or if he can,
It's thus he does it of a winter night.

# A Patch of Old Snow

There's a patch of old snow in a corner
    That I should have guessed
Was a blow-away paper the rain
    Had brought to rest.

It is speckled with grime as if
    Small print overspread it,
The news of a day I've forgotten—
    If I ever read it.

# Birches

When I see birches bend to left and right
Across the lines of straighter darker trees,
I like to think some boy's been swinging them.
But swinging doesn't bend them down to stay
As ice-storms do. Often you must have seen them
Loaded with ice a sunny winter morning
After a rain. They click upon themselves
As the breeze rises, and turn many-colored
As the stir cracks and crazes their enamel.
Soon the sun's warmth makes them shed crystal shells
Shattering and avalanching on the snow-crust—
Such heaps of broken glass to sweep away
You'd think the inner dome of heaven had fallen.
They are dragged to the withered bracken by the load,
And they seem not to break; though once they are bowed
So low for long, they never right themselves:
You may see their trunks arching in the woods
Years afterwards, trailing their leaves on the ground
Like girls on hands and knees that throw their hair
Before them over their heads to dry in the sun.
But I was going to say when Truth broke in
With all her matter-of-fact about the ice-storm
I should prefer to have some boy bend them
As he went out and in to fetch the cows—
Some boy too far from town to learn baseball,
Whose only play was what he found himself,
Summer or winter, and could play alone.
One by one he subdued his father's trees
By riding them down over and over again
Until he took the stiffness out of them,
And not one but hung limp, not one was left

For him to conquer. He learned all there was
To learn about not launching out too soon
And so not carrying the tree away
Clear to the ground. He always kept his poise
To the top branches, climbing carefully
With the same pains you use to fill a cup
Up to the brim, and even above the brim.
Then he flung outward, feet first, with a swish,
Kicking his way down through the air to the ground.
So was I once myself a swinger of birches.
And so I dream of going back to be.
It's when I'm weary of considerations,
And life is too much like a pathless wood
Where your face burns and tickles with the cobwebs
Broken across it, and one eye is weeping
From a twig's having lashed across it open.
I'd like to get away from earth awhile
And then come back to it and begin over.
May no fate willfully misunderstand me
And half grant what I wish and snatch me away
Not to return. Earth's the right place for love:
I don't know where it's likely to go better.
I'd like to go by climbing a birch tree,
And climb black branches up a snow-white trunk
*Toward* heaven, till the tree could bear no more,
But dipped its top and set me down again.
That would be good both going and coming back.
One could do worse than be a swinger of birches.

# The Hill Wife

LONELINESS
*(Her Word)*

One ought not to have to care
    So much as you and I
Care when the birds come round the house
    To seem to say good-by;

Or care so much when they come back
    With whatever it is they sing;
The truth being we are as much
    Too glad for the one thing

As we are too sad for the other here—
    With birds that fill their breasts
But with each other and themselves
    And their built or driven nests.


HOUSE FEAR

Always—I tell you this they learned—
Always at night when they returned
To the lonely house from far away
To lamps unlighted and fire gone gray,
They learned to rattle the lock and key
To give whatever might chance to be
Warning and time to be off in flight:
And preferring the out- to the in-door night,
They learned to leave the house-door wide
Until they had lit the lamp inside.

THE SMILE
*(Her Word)*

I didn't like the way he went away.
That smile! It never came of being gay.

Still he smiled—did you see him?—I was sure!
Perhaps because we gave him only bread
And the wretch knew from that that we were poor.
Perhaps because he let us give instead
Of seizing from us as he might have seized.
Perhaps he mocked at us for being wed,
Or being very young (and he was pleased
To have a vision of us old and dead).
I wonder how far down the road he's got.
He's watching from the woods as like as not.


THE OFT-REPEATED DREAM

She had no saying dark enough
    For the dark pine that kept
Forever trying the window-latch
    Of the room where they slept.

The tireless but ineffectual hands
    That with every futile pass
Made the great tree seem as a little bird
    Before the mystery of glass!

It never had been inside the room,
    And only one of the two
Was afraid in an oft-repeated dream
    Of what the tree might do.

## THE IMPULSE

It was too lonely for her there,
 And too wild,
And since there were but two of them,
 And no child,

And work was little in the house,
 She was free,
And followed where he furrowed field,
 Or felled tree.

She rested on a log and tossed
 The fresh chips,
With a song only to herself
 On her lips.

And once she went to break a bough
 Of black alder.
She strayed so far she scarcely heard
 When he called her—

And didn't answer—didn't speak—
 Or return.
She stood, and then she ran and hid
 In the fern.

He never found her, though he looked
 Everywhere,
And he asked at her mother's house
 Was she there.

Sudden and swift and light as that
    The ties gave,
And he learned of finalities
    Besides the grave.

# 'Out, Out—'

The buzz-saw snarled and rattled in the yard
And made dust and dropped stove-length sticks of wood,
Sweet-scented stuff when the breeze drew across it.
And from there those that lifted eyes could count
Five mountain ranges one behind the other
Under the sunset far into Vermont.
And the saw snarled and rattled, snarled and rattled,
As it ran light, or had to bear a load.
And nothing happened: day was all but done.
Call it a day, I wish they might have said
To please the boy by giving him the half hour
That a boy counts so much when saved from work.
His sister stood beside them in her apron
To tell them 'Supper.' At the word, the saw,
As if to prove saws knew what supper meant,
Leaped out at the boy's hand, or seemed to leap—
He must have given the hand. However it was,
Neither refused the meeting. But the hand!
The boy's first outcry was a rueful laugh,
As he swung toward them holding up the hand
Half in appeal, but half as if to keep
The life from spilling. Then the boy saw all—
Since he was old enough to know, big boy
Doing a man's work, though a child at heart—
He saw all spoiled. 'Don't let him cut my hand off
The doctor, when he comes. Don't let him, sister!'
So. But the hand was gone already.
The doctor put him in the dark of ether.
He lay and puffed his lips out with his breath.
And then—the watcher at his pulse took fright.
No one believed. They listened at his heart.

Little—less—nothing!—and that ended it.
No more to build on there. And they, since they
Were not the one dead, turned to their affairs.

# THE
# LEGACY

◆

# DONALD SHEEHAN

## The Frost Place

When in 1915 Robert Frost purchased a farm in Franconia, New Hampshire, he was forty years old and still unpublished in America. Five years later he had published two books and written most of his third, *New Hampshire*, which in 1923 would win the Pulitzer Prize. The second of these three books he called *Mountain Interval* (1916), to describe something of his life in the White Mountains of northern New Hampshire.

Houses and rooms are important to poets and their poems. James Merrill reminds us that the word *room* in Italian is *stanza*, and that how we fit our lives into the particular rooms we inhabit profoundly influences how we fit our words and sentences into the stanzas of our poems. Furthermore, the landscape into which a house fits equally informs a poet's work. Frost walked the hills and woods and roads here, and hiked the mountain trails, in what appears to have been a kind of contemplative practice of silent attentiveness. But always the long walks ended back in the low, white nineteenth-century farmhouse whose rooms contained all his family's love and suffering and delicacy and rage: sometimes just barely contained, one guesses. And in these rooms where he lived, Frost learned to fit the words of his family and farm and mountains and state into the stanzas of his poems, his sentences taking perfect shape, everything falling into place, as if the very rooms were showing him how. For some eighteen years after he left Franconia in 1920, he would return here in summer. His mountain interval had ended, but its meanings would carry through all his life.

In March 1976 the people of Franconia voted at town meeting to buy Frost's old farm and create The Frost Place, a museum and center for poetry and the arts. For the past twenty-four years, poets have come each summer to live and work in the rooms that once were Frost's. The richness and depth of the poems they have contributed to this book speak variously yet consonantly of our lives' rooms and landscapes. The poems are printed here in the order in which the poets arrived in Franconia, with Katha Pollitt first, in 1977, and Mark Cox most recently, in 2000. Each arrived as Frost did, with significant work accomplished (if not yet acknowledged), and each adapted to summer in a tiny mountain village (population 750) with characteristic intelligence, wit, and pleasure. The practical results of these mountain intervals may not yet be apparent, if ever they will be. But, in the meantime, the twenty-four poets of The Frost Place offer us these very beautiful poems and essays. And that is enough; indeed, it is wonderfully more than enough.

Since the beginning of the residency program in 1977, the Frost Place Board of Trustees has followed a consistent policy of choosing a poet from somewhere in America whose career in poetry at the time of the residency resembles Robert Frost's in 1915 when he arrived in Franconia: he had accomplished significant work (*A Boy's Will* and *North of Boston* had been published in England and were both about to be published in America by Henry Holt and Company), but he was not yet a famous figure in poetry. Chosen by the Board (a poet cannot apply for it), the resident poet has few duties and much unencumbered time in which to write. In his time in Franconia, Frost wrote many of his most famous lyrics; and he went from modest recognition to genuine fame in this period from 1915 to 1920. And during the summers from 1920 to 1938, he would return as often as he could to live and write in this nineteenth-century New England farmhouse that he came to love. The Board's hope is that the resident will find the summer as productive and lovely as Frost himself did.

Poet and editor Peter Davison of the *Atlantic Monthly* selected the first five poets, and I have chosen the poets since 1982. Two poets have advised me over the years in my choices: Sydney Lea, who chaired both Frost Place boards from 1993 through 1998, and Cleopatra Mathis, who was resident poet in 1982 and who has continued to serve on both boards since then. I am very grateful to them both.

Finally, the book's dedication to the people of Franconia indicates some of the Frost Place's immense gratitude to the town. Their decision in March 1976 to honor the significant literary past is as rare in any town's history as it is admirable. As Frost wrote in his long poem, "New Hampshire," he left southern New England to come to the White Mountains of New Hampshire, harboring no illusions about the people there being better than those he left: "I thought they couldn't be. And yet they were."

*—Donald Sheehan*
*Executive Director*
*The Frost Place*
*Franconia, New Hampshire*
*August 2000*

# MARY RUEFLE

## Frost Day Remarks

I grew up in a house without poetry. In 1962, when I was ten years old, my mother suffered a cerebral hemorrhage. It was assumed she was going to die, but she did not, and while she was in the hospital recovering from her brain surgery my father brought her a copy of Frost's *In the Clearing*, which had come out that year. And so a book of poetry entered our house. I didn't read it, though I loved poetry; by the time I was ready to take a long look at the adult world of poems, it was René Char and Henri Michaux and other "weird French poets" that I read. Two years ago my mother died, and I now own her copy of *In the Clearing*, inscribed to her by my father.

When I was nineteen I moved to Vermont and met a mechanic in a bar who was the son of Frost's biographer Laurence Thompson, and this young man regaled me with stories of being taught as a boy how to swing birches by the master himself. But that didn't sway me; I always suspected it was just an original way to pick up girls.

Ten years later—I still hadn't read much of Frost beyond the dozen most widely read and anthologized poems—I was hired as the caretaker of The Gulley, Frost's South Shaftsbury home, which had been bought by a television producer as a third home, and though the new owners came to Vermont only twice a year, in October and at Christmas, they loved the place, which was also on the National Register of Historic Places, and spoke of not changing a thing. Today the house has been so altered and expanded—it sleeps nearly forty, has a media center, a screening room, a pool, a hot tub, a satellite dish, new contours to the landscape, new ponds, and barns and buildings disproportionately high in plate glass—that it is no longer allowed to be on the historic register, and the brass plaque has been removed.

But when I lived there—and I lived there for ten years—it was roughly the same, and I lived in a corn crib that had been converted to a cottage where Frost, it is said, went to write. And it was there, in the cottage where he wrote many of his poems, that I read the poems, all of them, one long summer—if New England can be said to have long summers—and I understood at last what others had always known: Frost is an American master.

By then I was on speaking terms with his presence, and he still irked me, and I know I irked him, and our relationship remained mainly ironic until one year I went to China to teach. I missed New England sorely, especially in October, and while reading to my students "After Apple Picking," I felt, as I say in a poem that incorporates that moment, "like a discalced penitent." I was profoundly humbled and I remain so, but not without giving up my right to stand. Frost and I, we irk each other and love each other and most certainly follow each other around: that I am here at The Frost Place seems lovely and irksome and natural to me. When I first arrived at The Gulley, Frost's original mailbox was in the barn, his name hand-painted in his handwriting, all of it askew and rusting and shot though with buckshot holes—not all of his neighbors liked him it seems—and I was a poet and my friends were poets but for some reason it never occurred to me to keep the box, so when the groundskeeper came to me and said *what are we going to do with the mailbox* I said *oh, take it, sell it*, and he sold it the next day for ten dollars. And I have rued that day, though not so much as some of my friends who shake their heads and roll their eyes when they consider the gift I might have given *them*, for free.

When I drove up and saw the mailbox on Ridge Road, I felt at home, especially when Frost said to me "You see, irksome Mary, I'll be around long after you and all your attempts to get rid of me are gone."

Last fall I left Vermont after twenty-seven years, and moved to Amherst, Massachusetts. When I found the apartment I would eventually move into, my landlady pointed out the fabulous view from the kitchen window and said "There is where the Robert Frost Trail begins."

That's how it is with Frost and me: we talk, argue, play jokes on one another (I have a series of photographs of absurd plastic figures on his grave), bore each other, grow tired of each other, but keep being thrown together and are growing fond of our fate, for in this wild and dangerous life it is a good thing, to be thrown together with someone you recognize.

—*Mary Ruefle*
*Resident Poet 1999*

# SHARON BRYAN

## The Sound of Poetry

I remember Don Sheehan's phone call inviting me to be poet-in-residence at The Frost Place as vividly as I do the one saying my first book of poems had been accepted for publication: my hands wet from washing dishes, the wood grains in the desk swirling at right angles to those in the floor, the impatience in my voice—*Yes? Can I help you?* Then the gift: *We would like... Will you?* And the body accepting it: joy blooming like an enormous rose in my chest, the feet doing a little dance. Finally the voice: *Oh, yes.*

What I didn't say was that the invitation was more than a pleasure and an honor—it was a rescue.

I'd known about The Frost Place since it had been opened as a bicentennial project. Indeed, I thought they should somehow have known to invite me as its first resident, based on my love of Frost's poems, even though I hadn't yet published any work of my own. In the years since, I had published two books of poems, written a third, and been hired by a university to teach poetry—I thought I had finally accomplished the task Frost had set for himself in "Two Tramps in Mud Time": *My object in living is to unite / My avocation and my vocation / As my two eyes make one in sight....* I thought I could sustain that vision for the rest of my life.

But before my third book found a publisher, the first two went out of print. At the same time, there were other losses: friends, a lover, a beloved city. At first the writing had consoled me, but when none of it was in print I began to lose faith in writing poetry as a way to make sense of life and death, as my way of being in and of the world. I had a sort of tantrum: I refused to listen to the voices that had spoken poems to me, refused to write down what they said—and eventually I no longer heard them.

◆

Not long afterwards, I had decided to leave the city where I'd never felt at home, where I'd lost my sense of who and what I was and had fallen into such despair. I'd quit my teaching job and begun to pack all my belongings without knowing where I would go. Then I had gotten the phone call. At a time when I wasn't at all sure who I was or whether I'd ever write poems again, I'd been given at least a temporary identity and home: poet-in-residence.

By the time I left for The Frost Place, everything I owned was in storage in Memphis—I would send for it when I had a more permanent place to live. I'd left before, every chance I got, but this time my cat Mirabelle was in her carrier on the seat next to me, and I was never going back. I cranked up the volume and sang along at the top of my lungs with Janis Joplin. *Take it, take another little piece of my heart now....* Even she sounded joyful.

◆

As I drove north, away from the place where I'd been so unhappy, I was thinking about all I'd left behind, in Memphis and before that. Some things I'd left with pleasure—I liked traveling light—and some with regret. I thought of Odysseus trying to explain to everyone, including himself, how it was he'd come to be alone and empty-handed.

At the same time, a passage from one of the essays in a book I had just edited (*Where We Stand: Women Poets on Literary Tradition*) kept replaying in my head: *Of course I had inherited a highly romantic, male notion of the artist, a being untethered by domestic concerns, but I didn't know that yet. I didn't know there were alternatives.* How blithe the writer's past tense is, how impatient with her younger, naive self. When I'd first read those sentences, they had taken my breath away, had rippled back through my life and the choices I'd made.

I'd realized immediately that not only had I inherited that notion of the artist, but that I had built my life around it. Growing up I had sometimes imagined becoming a doctor, and I'd been stunned to realize, years later, that in those scenes I had always pictured myself as a male doctor. Now I was chagrined to think I might also have made the same mistake when I envisioned my life as a poet.

I may not have seen any women doctors as a child, but I certainly knew examples of women poets—first in books, and then when I met them and heard them read their poems. The women writers whose lives first came to mind—Dickinson, Moore, Bishop—all had the same shape: unmarried, no children. Browning had been married but had no children; Dinesen had been married and divorced. Plath had been a wife and mother, but she hadn't survived. I took their renunciations as part of the price of a writer's life. How had I managed to ignore all the examples of women writers who did have husbands and children? Why hadn't I ever seen myself when I looked at them? As I went over the list of contributors to the book, I realized that about half of them had children. Some of my writer friends had children. I had to have known it was possible—just not for me.

*I cannot live with you*, Dickinson says to a man she loves, and I had said that more than once: to my high school boyfriend, to a husband, a lover. I'd never seen marriage and children in the same picture with any career, so I certainly hadn't imagined combining them with being a writer, and even when I had most wanted a baby, I had never wanted a child full-time. I love the pleasures of my solitary life: hours of uninterrupted reading, following a thought, listening to music, writing whenever I want, the little daily routines. Maybe all our theories arise out of our temperaments: I love solitude, therefore writing requires that I live alone.

So why did those few words from the essay make me call my whole life into question? Because I have indeed put everything into writing's one basket. I have family—my parents, two brothers, aunts, uncles, cousins. I have friends, students, colleagues. They're all enormously important to me, crucial to my life. But I've staked my life on writing. If it fails me, or if I fail it, my life will have texture but no meaning—I could be adrift *nineteen times as high as the moon*. I read that essay at a point when I had lost my faith in writing poetry, and didn't know if it would ever return. I was editing the essays because they mattered to me, but also as a way to stay in motion. And then one of them told me—too late—that maybe I could have lived my life differently.

◆

When I was in college, taking a seminar on Frost's poetry, a friend and I decided that we'd make a pilgrimage to visit Frost that coming summer. Neither of us had been east of Chicago, let alone to New England. We didn't know exactly where Frost lived, didn't have any money for a trip, and had to work to pay for school, so this was probably more a fantasy than a plan. But it was never put to the test because Frost died that January—I was so crushed my friend sent me a sympathy card.

Now, years later, I was not only going to Frost's house, but staying there. When I'd first begun reading contemporary poetry, I was a little embarrassed in retrospect at how much I had loved Frost's work. I had been naive about so many things—why not that too? His poems were old-fashioned, probably simplistic and sentimental—at least that's what I feared. I protected my earlier memories by not going back to look. Eventually, though, I'd been away long enough that it seemed safe to read them again—and of course when I did, I could see more complexity in their darkness, more subtlety in their technique. It was like meeting a friend you haven't seen in years and discovering you have even more in common than you did the first time around.

I understood now, though, that the work was the only place we could meet, and that even if my friend and I had somehow managed to find Frost years earlier, the visit would have been a disaster and a disappointment. I knew this was much better luck, to be going to his house when he no longer lived there.

The house in Franconia, New Hampshire, is the one the family moved into soon after they came back from England, where Frost had finally managed to have his first books of poems published and to embark on what was to be his very public literary career. They lived first in another house on the same road, but Frost thought this one had a better view of the White Mountains and bullied the farmer who owned it into selling it to him. The house is two-story but small, and its best feature is the porch running almost the width of the front, facing the mountains. Downstairs there's a living room divided by an oversize fireplace, a small kitchen, bedroom, bathroom, and Frost's study. A screened porch at the back looks into the woods. Upstairs are three small bedrooms. There's an old well just outside the kitchen door, a beautiful barn a hundred yards up from the house, and then, winding through the woods, a recently added poetry trail: a path through wildflowers and trees with individual poems on plaques along the way.

The coal stove Frost's wife Elinor used still took up a third of the kitchen, but I was warned not to try to use it. Elinor's piano, badly out of tune, stood against a living room wall. I hadn't taken piano lessons since I was fifteen, and I'd never been more than a mediocre beginner, but my first week there I bought a children's book of Sunday school songs so I could pick out the melodies. When I played, Mirabelle scrambled down from the couch and stalked into the bedroom.

I hadn't really had a choice about bringing her with me—she was thirteen years old, diabetic, and needed a shot of insulin each morning. When I'd gotten her as a kitten I'd named her after a character in James Merrill's *Changing Light at Sandover*, and *Mirabelle* seemed to summon a kind of demonic spirit—my housesitters referred to her as *the cat from hell*. She terrorized Harriet, the wonderful cat I thought she'd be a companion for, bit people who tried to pet her, ran around the walls at night. I thought more than once about returning her to the shelter, but could never quite bring myself to do it. When Harriet died, ten years later, Mirabelle seemed to come into her own, as if she'd been waiting her whole life to be an only cat. A year after that she'd been diagnosed with diabetes, lost half her body weight, and almost died before she'd leveled off at five pounds. I admired her tenacity, her refusal to go gentle into any sort of night.

Mirabelle was like a surly little person in a cat suit, and seemed to have no cat instincts. She killed bugs dutifully but reluctantly with one swipe—no toying with them—then drank a whole saucer of water to clear her palate. She speared her Tender Vittles, then ate them delicately, one a time, from her claws. The only time I had taken her outside she had scratched my shoulder until it bled, and had never even looked out the window after that.

But the first day we were at Frost's house, as I was standing by the kitchen screen door, she rubbed against my leg and mewed to go out. *Don't be ridiculous*, I said. And then I thought, *Why not?* I opened the door, and she walked cautiously onto the grass—then jumped back. She tried again, this time keeping to the stepping stones. Not so bad. She walked slowly around the back of the house, up to the barn. I stayed right behind, ready to grab her if I saw any danger. She seemed more bemused than curious—*what an odd house, so many rooms*.

After that she usually came with me on the poetry trail, keeping carefully to the path. I left her in the house when I went to town in the afternoons, but soon discovered she mewed at the tourists until they let her out. Once she got outside, she had no idea what to do, so when I drove up in the evening she'd be sitting hidden in the wildflowers that edged the porch, like a little tiger in a Rousseau painting. I was touched by the late blossoming, by her discovery of a whole new world.

◆

The prettiest room in the house is Frost's study, with his desk, a photograph of the handsome young poet, cases displaying manuscripts, a rocking chair. I sat where Frost had sat, leaned my elbows on his desk, traced his handwriting. Friends asked if I saw Frost's ghost. No, I said, but I heard him almost constantly.

*The line-storm clouds fly tattered and swift, / The road is forlorn all day / Where a myriad snowy quartz stones lift / And the hoofprints vanish away. / The roadside flower, too wet for the bee / Expends her bloom in vain / —Come over the hills and far with me / And be my love in the rain.* I've always longed to have great quantities of poetry by heart, but in fact I have a bad memory. Frost's poems are some of the only ones that settled in and still rise whole to the surface. *Love at the lips was touch / As sweet as I could bear, / And once that seemed too much, / I lived on air....* The words weren't just in my ears, but in my whole body as I walked, almost as deep as nursery rhymes.

A little shelf on the stair landing holds a book open to Frost's most familiar poem, "The Road Not Taken." When I was in the house I could hear tourists quoting the ending to each other as if it were a motto for how we should live: *Two roads diverged in a wood, and I— / I took the one less traveled by / And that has made all the difference.* As I took my coffee out onto the poetry trail one morning, with Mirabelle close behind, I thought about reading the poem with my students and watching them realize what a misreading that is.

In fact, the roads in the poem are virtually identical. I stopped on the path to read the lines again: *... long I stood / And looked down one as far as I could / To where it bent in the undergrowth;/ Then took the other, as just as fair, / And having perhaps the better claim, / Because it was grassy and wanted wear; / Though as for that the passing there / Had worn them really about the same.* The speaker is looking for a difference between them, a reason to take one or the other, and tries out the notion of one being less traveled—but he decides even that's not true, and finally has to do the equivalent of a mental coin flip: *And both that morning equally lay / In leaves no step had trodden black. / Oh, I kept the first for another day! / Yet knowing how way leads on to way, / I doubted if I should ever come back.*

Mirabelle rubbed against my leg to urge me forward, but I was still thinking about the poem. This is a speaker who understands human psychology, including his own. We have to make choices, but we're reluctant to admit how large a role chance and accident play. So we invent reasons after the fact to explain to ourselves and others how we got where we are, to make the stories of our lives more rational and shapely than our actual lives ever can be: *I shall be telling this with a sigh / Somewhere ages and ages hence: / Two roads diverged in a wood, and I— / I took the one less traveled by, / And that has made all the difference.*

It's that colon after *hence* that's crucial: this will be my story, this is the reason I'll come up with to explain the inexplicable. He even knows the tone and gesture he will use: *I shall be telling this with a sigh.* It isn't a cynical confession—well, I know I'll lie about this, and here's how—but an account of how life gets transformed into the story of our lives and sometimes into art.

Mirabelle had been mewing impatiently while I stood there reading and thinking, unwilling to wander off on her own. When I bent down to pet her I was surprised, as I always was, by how bony she felt through her long fur. I stepped back onto the trail to follow its simple, unbranched circle—no choices to make except whether to keep going or turn back. Another image of roads came to mind, from *Out of Africa*. Dinesen repeats a story she was told as a child, one where the teller drew pictures to accompany the story as it went along. The plot is simple: a man is wakened at night by a tremendous noise and sets off in the dark to find out what caused it. He keeps stumbling and falling, and only after he's done this many times does he discover that the noise was made when a dam broke on his pond, letting all the water rush out. He repairs the leak, goes back to bed, sleeps through the night. In the morning, when he looks out his upstairs window, he sees that his nighttime journey, what had seemed like random accidents, has the shape of a stork.

Dinesen comforts herself with this story during the worst time of her life, when she's losing everything she cares about: her coffee farm, her African friends, her lover. *The tight place, the dark pit in which I am now lying, of what bird is it the talon? When the design of my life is completed, shall I, shall other people see a stork?* I can't quite give up the fantasy of seeing my own skeleton; I have a hard time letting go of the notion that I can see the design of my life before it's completed. And yet I know Frost was right and Dinesen wrong: there is no fixed shape, just way leading on to way—more of a scrawl than a stork.

I know the shape of this walk I'm on with my cat, but what does she see except grass waving on either side of her, bugs she steps around, my shoes rising and falling ahead of her, and a too bright light when she looks up to be petted?

Even if I'd already been working on poems when I arrived, I doubt that I could have kept on while I stayed there. I was thrilled to have been asked, but actually living in the house was a mixed blessing. The barn, parts of the house, and the poetry trail were open to visitors every afternoon, and I soon discovered there was no place in the house where I could be out of sight and sound when they were going through. And, it turned out, I wasn't safe from interruption even when the house was supposedly closed to visitors. A large sign on the front lawn listed the afternoon hours the house was open and urged visitors to respect the poet's privacy at other times. Even so, a couple banged on the screen door early one morning when I was eating my cereal, and one day when I was in bed with a migraine a woman barged in to ask if she could use the bathroom. One night someone pounded on the front door until I got out of the tub, put on a robe, and went to the door, assuming there was an emergency. A tall, imperious man said he was passing through, this was the only time he could see the place, I must let him in. I thought of the father in a Ring Lardner story addressing his son: *Shut up, he explained.* No, he couldn't come in, I explained, and slammed the door. It was indeed horrible, even by proxy, to be *public, like a frog.*

But when I took my coffee through the woods in the morning or sat on the porch in the evening, the place was idyllic, magical. That's when I heard Frost's voice and my own thoughts and fell under the power of the landscape. I listened to the crickets and looked at the stars and felt both awed and peaceful.

And of course many of the visitors were as pleased to be there as I was, and respectful of the surroundings. One day, while I was still looking for a place in the house where I could work without being seen, I was sitting on the screened porch just a few feet from the stairway. I could hear a mother and daughter talking—the girl was nine or ten, she wrote poems herself, she was thrilled to be in Frost's house. Her mother urged her not to talk too loudly since a poet was living in the house. The daughter's voice dropped to a rapturous whisper: *Oh! Do you think if I keep writing that maybe someday when I grow up I might get to stay here?* I almost leapt out from my hiding place. *Yes, yes you can. That's exactly what happened to me.*

◆

I knew how lucky I was to be meeting Frost this way, obliquely—with just the door ajar between us, as Dickinson says—rather than firsthand, in person, as I had hoped to in college. Even if my friend and I had managed to make the trip, had found him, what would we have said to him, and he to us? He was an old man, often curmudgeonly, and we were naive kids, fans.

The place where we could meet without being distracted by our differences was in the poems. Frost the man wouldn't have given me the time of day. Frost the poet was a kindred spirit: we shared thoughts and feelings, a love for philosophical questions: *What brought the . . . spider to that height, / Then steered the white moth thither in the night? / What but design of darkness to appall?— / If design govern in a thing so small.* I don't know of a scarier line of poetry than that last one, offered not *with a sigh*, but almost as an afterthought: would you really want to believe in a god who supervises the minutest details of death?

But the voice in the poem is not the person, any more than the faces I conjured listening to my favorite shows as a child were the faces of the actors I saw in *Radio Mirror*. When a friend told me she'd met Elizabeth Bishop I said, *Oh, you were so lucky*, forgetting for a moment that I'd met Bishop myself. I'd accompanied the man I was living with to a small dinner given for her at another poet's house. I'd never even seen a full-length photo of Bishop at the time, and I pictured her as tall, slim, patrician. So I was startled to meet a short, round-faced woman dressed in cruise wear. She'd just gotten out of the hospital and was still very tired, but she did fifteen minutes of brilliant conversation. Then, only a few minutes into dinner, her friend Alice excused herself to take Bishop upstairs. Bishop was both ill and drunk, and leaned heavily on Alice as they left the table. I forget that I met her because I don't feel as if I met the person who speaks the poems I love.

I realized, one day when I was reading and making some notes in the little Franconia library, that I write to make a better self—just as I imagine Bishop did. If I stop writing I'm left with my worst selves, untransformed. One of Bishop's best known poems is a villanelle, "One Art." It's an instruction manual: *The art of losing isn't hard to master. . . . / Lose something every day.* Her advice is to start small: *lost door keys, the hour badly spent.* But that's just the beginning: *Then practice losing farther, losing faster: places, and names, and where it was you meant to travel. . . . my mother's watch . . . three loved houses.* The losses get bigger: *two cities, lovely ones . . . two rivers, a continent.* These are all leading up to the greatest loss of all: *Even losing you (the joking voice, a gesture I love . . .).* Practice makes perfect, she's managed what might have seemed impossible: *It's evident the art of losing's not too hard to master / though it may look like (*Write it!*) like disaster.* The pain is palpable, but managed, shaped, transformed by art and into art.

Not long ago a friend described to me the drafts that led up to "One Art," and they're everything the poem is not: whiny, self-pitying, angry, chaotic. There's a swirl of emotions, some bad lines, and then, gradually, all of that begins to take on more shape, Bishop finally tries the villanelle form, and the poem's voice begins to emerge.

I think that's what she was writing and waiting for, to hear that voice that's both hers and not hers, a public voice that's meant to be heard— or overheard—by someone else. It's different from the private voice, the voice of gossip, diaries, daily conversation. It isn't simply a matter of putting a good face on things—though I suppose that's part of it. It's not at all that the private voice is emotional and the public one rational. And I wouldn't describe the tone in Bishop's poem as one of *emotions recollected in tranquility.* It isn't tranquil at all, but heartbroken, crushed, devastated.

I can use all those adjectives exactly because she doesn't. If she had stopped at one of the earlier drafts, and called that the poem, I would have responded with impatience rather than sympathy. The finished poem doesn't simply describe those messier, less appealing emotions; it transforms them—for the reader and the writer.

Writing isn't therapy, though they have some things in common. In therapy Bishop might have brought her feelings to the surface in order to see them, acknowledge them, and let them go. By writing the poem she used those same emotions as fuel that launched the poem and then burned away, leaving the made thing, the work of art. And when the poem was finished, its emotions became her emotions: when she looked in its mirror she saw her *doppelgänger*, a better self. Not a perfect self, but a self who could make something out of loss instead of being undone by it. She wrote the poem in order to become the person capable of saying what it says. All writers have these shadow selves that flicker through the work like birds glimpsed through the trees: sometimes you can see them when you read between the lines.

◆

At night I sat on the porch, staring into the dark and thinking about the shape of my life. I was a poet with no books. I had no husband and no children. I had become exactly what I'd been determined to avoid: an old maid schoolteacher. A spinster who couldn't spin. Dante's words— or at least their English version—had been echoing in my head since I had so thoroughly lost sight of myself in Memphis: *I found myself, midlife, in the middle of a dark wood.* It's one of those strange accidents of language that *lost* and *found* described the same moment. I had lost myself in a dark wood, but I seemed to be working my way out of it. I'd certainly felt as if I were living in exile in Memphis, and in my own personal hell. Maybe after I'd seen every level I would make my way gradually up, first to purgatory and then to paradise.

I wanted to believe in that shape—it's the stuff of fairy tales, after all: first the trials and tribulations, then the happy ending. But I'd found myself in dark woods before, made my way out, gotten lost again. I knew happiness wasn't a state I could simply move to and live in forever. I thought of my favorite Frost title, "Happiness Makes Up in Height for What It Lacks in Length." *Oh, stormy stormy world*, it begins, and goes on to say that the clear days have been so few *I can but wonder whence / I get the lasting sense / Of so much warmth and light.* He thinks it may be *From one day's perfect weather,* when *No shadow crossed but ours / As through its blazing flowers / We went from house to wood / For change of solitude.* Everyone lives happily ever after in fairy tales because the stories end there, with one of those moments of happiness. Suppose the characters started to live happily ever after halfway through—what would the rest of the story be about?

So the shape of my life isn't a descent into hell followed by a glorious, blazing ascent. The despair is intermittent, and the happiness. Sometimes I wander into the woods and get lost, sometimes I drift too far to the other side of the path and slip down a cliff. It seems more like the life of the character in Dinesen's story—the falling down and getting up. But I think if I could look out the window at it I wouldn't see a stork or any other single, fixed design—I don't believe in that kind of a god. I think it's more like an ink blot, and I can see this story in it, and that, and that. Or like looking at the stars overhead and connecting a few in constellations.

How much of my life is choice, and how much chance? I live alone because I love solitude, because I'm married to poetry; I live alone because I never had the feeling my friend describes on meeting the man who became her husband—*Oh, there you are.* I don't have children because I never wanted to take care of them twenty-four hours a day; I don't have children because I was never with the right man, because I never got pregnant. I write poems because I choose to; I write poems because I'm driven to. The road forks, I go one way or the other. And Frost's right: *Yet knowing how way leads on to way, / I doubted if I should ever come back.* Even when I changed my mind about some things, there was no going back.

Stephen J. Gould describes the one-wayness of evolution: at every point along the way, life could have taken the other fork in the road, the one leading to other ways. If the whole process could be started again from the beginning, it would be impossible to end with life as we know it now—there are too many other alternatives; chance is too big a factor. Flip a coin: no life on land. Flip a coin: no vertebrates. Flip a coin: no mammals. Do that for every small and large detail along the way. Beautiful unfoldings and layerings, but not with any end in mind. Flip a coin: no minds pondering these questions.

Any god could have designed a better system for walking on two legs than the human spine, but evolution doesn't start with a blank slate, it has to work with what's already there. In this case it had to work with a spine shaped by animals that walked on four legs, animals that swung through the trees. I revise my life as I go along, but I have to work with what's already there. Newer understandings may complicate old habits, but they won't ever erase them. Leaving a destructive relationship didn't buy back the years of my life I'd spent in it. Seeing that I followed a male model for my life as a poet wouldn't bring me a daughter now, even if I wanted one.

Maybe my life looks like a leafy cottonwood. Instead of lying in a bird's talon, as Dinesen was, there I am at the tip of a small twig. Rilke says, over and over in every poet's head, *You must change your life*, and when I was young I thought that meant something like, *Become a different kind of tree*. Or, seal up one room and move on to the next, like the chambered nautilus. Now I think it means, *Keep going, but don't think you can always choose what you'll take with you and what you'll leave behind*. Writing is what I do in response to Rilke's challenge: if I were totally happy with who I am and what I know, I wouldn't need to write.

◆

During the August writers' conference at The Frost Place there were morning talks in the barn, workshops in the house during the day, and readings at night back in the barn. Mirabelle visited the workshops, getting petted and sniffing backpacks, but I usually left her in the house during the morning talks. When Hayden Carruth spoke, he began with a brief excerpt of Billie Holliday singing. *Notice this little moan she makes at the beginning*, he said. *That's what poetry comes out of, that wordless feeling*. He played it again, then went on with his talk. As he concluded, he returned to the notion of the silence that precedes poetry. He was leading up to playing the Billie Holliday one more time. *What's the sound we want?* he asked. And before he could play the tape, a piercing single note made us all turn our heads: Mirabelle standing in the open barn door.

After I'd packed to leave, I sat at Frost's desk one last time, then in the rocking chair. What would he have made of me? Not much, but it didn't matter. I was there in his house, listening to his poems, looking at what he saw, but he was behind me in the past—or he'd gone over the falls of time ahead of me. The linguist Benjamin Whorf distinguished Hopi spots of time from our linear image of an arrow speeding only one way. In Hopi time, he said, there's this time, and this time, and this time—separate little ponds, not an onrushing river. Memory seems to work that way, but not life itself. Life runs through our hands like water; a poem is a net that saves a few bits and pieces while the rest is sluiced away. A poem is a net that breaks my fall.

My stay at The Frost Place had restored my hearing, restored me to poetry, as if I had drunk deep from the well at the side of the house. I thought of the ending of Frost's poem "Directive," lines I had once imagined engraving on my poetry bookcases: *Here are your waters and your watering place, / Drink and be whole again beyond confusion.* I didn't expect ever to be beyond confusion—and didn't think I wanted to be. But I did feel whole again, and ready to listen.

—*Sharon Bryan*
*Resident Poet, 1993*

# THE
# RESIDENT POETS

◆

# KATHA POLLITT

## 1977

In her poems, Katha Pollitt exhibits a fine intelligence joined to a lyrical freshness. The danger of mere intelligence is weariness; while mere lyricism too often has nowhere to go. Katha Pollitt achieves a lyrical renewal of what I shall call social intelligence: that gaze of the mind out upon our social pleasures and afflictions and deceptions. She does this by sheer loveliness of voice—a voice that, whether exasperated or impassioned, always takes the ear. Thus she brings to her poems an incisiveness that knows how to sing.

—Donald Sheehan

# Mind-Body Problem

When I think of my youth I feel sorry not for myself
but for my body. It was so direct
and simple, so rational in its desires,
wanting to be touched the way an otter
loves water, the way a giraffe
wants to amble the edge of the forest, nuzzling
the tender leaves at the tops of the trees. It seems
unfair, somehow, that my body had to suffer
because I, by which I mean my mind, was saddled
with certain unfortunate high-minded romantic notions
that made me tyrannize and patronize it
like a cruel medieval baron, or an ambitious
English-professor husband ashamed of his wife—
her love of sad movies, her budget casseroles
and regional vowels. Perhaps
my body would have liked to make some of our dates,
to come home at four in the morning and answer my scowl
with "None of your business!" perhaps
it would have liked more presents: silks, mascaras.
If we had had a more democratic arrangement
we might even have come, despite our different backgrounds
to a grudging respect for each other, like Tony Curtis
and Sidney Poitier fleeing handcuffed together,
instead of the current curious shift of power
in which I find I am being reluctantly
dragged along by my body as though by some
swift and powerful dog. How eagerly
it plunges ahead, not stopping for anything,
as though it knows exactly where we are going.

# Lives of the Nineteenth-Century Poetesses

As girls they were awkward and peculiar,
wept in church or refused to go at all.
Their mothers saw right away no man would marry them.
So they must live at the sufferance of others,
timid and queer as governesses out of Chekhov,
malnourished on theology, boiled eggs and tea,
but given to outbursts of pride that embarrass everyone.
After the final quarrel, the grand
renunciation, they retire upstairs to the attic
or to the small room in the cheap off-season hotel
and write *Today I burned all your letters* or
*I dreamed the magnolia blazed like an avenging angel*
*and when I woke I knew I was in Hell.*
No one is surprised when they die young,
having left all their savings to a wastrel nephew
to be remembered for a handful
of "minor but perfect" lyrics
a passion for jam or charades
and a letter still preserved in the family archives:
"I send you herewith the papers of your aunt
who died last Tuesday in the odor of sanctity
although a little troubled in her mind
by her habit, much disapproved of by the ignorant,
of writing down the secrets of her heart."

# Mandarin Oranges

I can't remember if I even liked them,
when they were the special treat of our high-school lunchroom.
Probably not—they smacked of bribery:

for chapel, volleyball and lima beans
this splash of the Orient in a thin sugary plasma.
and yet today at the supermarket I

saw that silly geisha flirt her fan
against the flat insipid turquoise sea
and wanted mandarin oranges more than

I've ever wanted anything, as if
they held the essence of youth and joy. O sweetness,
sunrise, hibiscus, Chinese lanterns, hearts—

we can't keep faith with the past,          .
in the end we love it because it is the past,
no matter how stubbornly we tell ourselves

"Remember what this was like,
how bored you were, how miserable." Inscribed
in a margin of Modern Chemistry and dated
March 15, 1965.

# Collectibles

Even jumbled here in the schoolyard rummage sale
they keep their spirits up. This battered tin
combination cheese-and-nutmeg shaver
still offers *"Gratings" from Fort Lauderdale*,
this bunch of velvet violets breathes a pale,
still-shocking scent of lingerie, and here
(but where's your mate? Your shiny silver cap?)
is—can it be?—the purple jug-shape blown-
glass salt shaker from my parents' kitchen table.
A manic friendliness infuses these
things that mostly look like other things—
the tomato that holds thread, the black-and-white
kitten teapot, one paw raised for spout—
like toys that in a child's dream play all night
or like the magic kitchens in cartoons
where pots and pans leap down from the shelf and dance
and the orange squeezer oompahs like a tuba.
Innocent, foolish, jaunty, trivial,
small travellers from a land that thought it was
so full of love and coziness and cheer
the least things shared in it—why should
they pain us so somehow, who know so well
it wasn't like that, not really, even then?
Is that what they have come so far to tell us?
that we lose even what we never had?

# Playground

In the hygienic sand
of the new municipal sandbox
children with names from the soaps
Brandon and Samantha
fill and empty, fill and empty
their bright plastic buckets
alongside children with names
from obscure books of the Bible.
we are all mothers here,
friendly and polite.
we are teaching our children to share.

A man could slice his way
through us like a pirate!
and why not? didn't we open
our bodies to any star, say
Little One, whoever you are, come in?
But the men are busy elsewhere.
Broadhipped, in fashionable sweatpants
we discuss the day—a tabloid
murder, does cold cream work?
those students in China

and as we talk, not one of us
isn't thinking, Mama, was it
like this? Did I do this to you?
But Mama too is busy,
she is dead, or in Florida
or taking up new interests
and the children want apple juice

and Cheerios, diapers and naps.
We have no one to ask but each other.
But we do not ask each other.

# Happiness Writes White

So what good is it? Let's be sad,
wear melancholy like an old brown sweater
patched at the elbows and smelling of our own funk.
The coffee cups pile up on the little table,
pages turn, electric lights come on—
it would be good to have a dog, you think,
one with grave eyes and an understanding of life,
it would be good

to go down to the docks and watch the freighters
idly listing in the oily water,
to smoke a cigarette and look out at the sea
and then walk home in the gathering evening,
at a measured pace, still hearing the voice of the sea
that speaks to you like a friend, of serious things
so simply and quietly
you barely notice the sky blanch after rain
or the woman coming out of the subway
carrying an immense bouquet of white lilac
wrapped in white tissue paper, like a torch.

# Dreaming About the Dead

You'd think they'd just been out for a casual stroll
and found themselves by chance on the old street,
the old key still in their pocket, the way

they're sitting at the kitchen table when you come in.
Don't you believe it. They've obviously spent hours
arranging for the light to fall with that

phony lambency,
and haven't you noticed how slyly
they look at you when they think you're not looking at them?

True, it seems strange that they would come so far
to warn you against the new girl in the office
or give you a recipe for worms on toast,

but try it, interrupt, say *mirror of ashes,*
*moonless heart*—they'll only
smile a little vaguely, start hunting for matches

and suddenly the black car's at the door.
will you come back? you call out after them.
Oh, definitely, no problem there. Again

and again, until
you learn they will never say what you need them to:
*My death was mine. It had nothing to do with you.*

# A Walk

When I go for a walk and see they're tearing down
some old red-plush Rialto for an office building
and suddenly realize this was where Mama and I
saw "Lovers of Teruel" three times in a single sitting

and the drugstore where we went afterwards for ice cream's
gone too, and Mama's gone and my ten-year-old self,
I admire more than ever the ancient Chinese poets
who were comforted in exile by thoughts of the transience of life

How *yesterday*, for instance, *quince bloomed in the Emperor's courtyard*
*but today wild geese fly south over ruined towers.*
Or, *Oh, full moon that shone on our scholarly wine parties,*
*do you see us now, scattered on distant shores?*

A melancholy restraint is surely the proper approach
to take in this world. And so I walk on, recall-
ing Hsin Ch'i-chi, who when old and full of sadness
wrote merely, "A cool day, a fine fall."

# Small Comfort

Coffee and cigarettes in a clean cafe,
forsythia lit like a damp match against
a thundery sky drunk on its own ozone,

the laundry cool and crisp and folded away
again in the lavender closet—too late to find
comfort enough in such small daily moments

of beauty, renewal, calm, too late to imagine
people would rather be happy than suffering
and inflicting suffering. We're near the end,

but O before the end, as the sparrows wing
each night to their secret nests in the elm's green dome
O let the last bus bring

lover to lover, let the starveling
dog turn the corner and lope suddenly
miraculously, down its own street, home.

# ROBERT HASS

## 1978

In his poems, Robert Hass explores what he calls, in a marvelous poem, the "privilege of being." By this he means that immensely graceful yet endlessly collapsing world of our relationships and especially our erotic lives: a world that at once exhalts and degrades us, healing one set of wounds by making another set, an equally rending and more deeply shameful set of fresh wounds. In his poems we seem to be always losing ground—and then comes the shock that illuminates everything: as we lose ground, we go deeper and still deeper into the capacity to love. His work contains surprising grace.

—Donald Sheehan

# At Squaw Valley

*—for Sharon Olds*

I don't even know which sadness
it was came up
in me when we were walking down the road to Shirley Lake,
the sun gleaming in snow patches,
the sky so blue it seemed the light's dove
of some pentecost of blue,
the mimulus, yellow, delicate of petal,
and the pale yellow cinquefoil trembling in the wet
air above the creek,
and fields of lupine,
that blue blaze of lupine, a swatch of paintbrush
sheening it—and so much of it, long meadows
of it gathered out of mountain air and spilling
down ridge toward the lake it almost looked like
in the wind. I think I must have thought
the usual things; that the flowering season
in these high mountain meadows, that
the feeling, something like hilarity, of sudden
pleasure when you first see some tough little plant
you knew you'd see comes because it seems—I mean
by *it* the larkspur or the penstemon curling
and arching the reach of its sexual being
up out of a little crack in granite—to say
that human hunger has a place up here in the light-cathedral
of the dazzled air. I wanted to tell you
that when the ghost-child died, the three-month dreamer
she and I would never know, I kept feeling that
the heaven it went to was like the inside of a store window
on a rainy day from which you watch blurred forms
passing in the street. Or to tell you, more terrible,

that when she and I walked off the restlessness
of our misery afterwards in the Coast Range hills,
we saw come out of the thicket shyly
a pure white doe. I wanted to tell you I knew
it was a freak of beauty like the law of averages
that killed our child and made us know, as you said,
that things between lovers, even of longest standing,
can fail in their bodies though their wits don't fail.
Not things, life. Still later on the beach,
we watched the waves. No two the same size,
no two in the same arch of rising up and pouring.
But it was the same law. You shell a pea,
there are three plump seeds and one that's shriveled.
You shell a bushelful and begin to feel the rhythm
of the waves at Limantour that last bright October day.
It killed something in me, or froze it,
to have to see where beauty came from. I imagined
for a long time that the baby, since
it would have liked to smell our clothes to know
what a mother and father would have been,
hovered sometimes in our closet and I half-expected
to see it there, half-fish spirit, form of tenderness,
a little dead dreamer with open eyes. That was
private sorrow. I didn't try to talk about it.
I found I couldn't write. I knew what two people
couldn't say
on a cold November morning in the fog—
you remember the feel of Berkeley winter mornings—
what they couldn't say to each other
was the white deer not seen. It meant to me
that beauty and terror were intertwined so powerfully
and went so deep that any kind of love
could fail. I didn't say it. Maybe there wasn't time.
We may have been sprinting to catch the tram

because we had to teach poetry
in that valley two thousand feet below us.
You were running—Gabe's mother, David's lover,
mother and lover (grieving) of a girl
about to leave for school and die to you a little
(or die into you: become, grandly, the person
every child knows their parent should have been)
you were running, dear one, like a gazelle,
in purple underpants, royal purple,
and I laughed out loud. It was the excess
the world gives, the more-than-you-bargained for
surprise of it, waves breaking,
the abundant, sudden fragrance of the mimulus at creekside.
Things bloom up there. They are,
for their season, alive in those bright epiphanies
of air we ran through.

# The Couple

Summoned by conscious recollection, she
would be smiling, they might be in a kitchen talking,
before or after dinner. But they are in this other room,
the window has many small panes, and they are on a couch,
embracing. Or, rather, he holds her as tightly
as he can, she buries herself in his body.
There is morning—maybe it is evening—light
flowing through the room, but outside
day is slowly succeeded by night
succeeded by day. Like a back projection of time passing,
the process wobbles wildly and accelerates:
weeks, months, years. The light in the room
does not change. This is how we come to the brokenness
of things. It is plain what is happening.
They are trying to become one creature,
and something will not have it. Oh, they are tender
with each other. Their hunger is sexual,
though they will not let it give them peace. They are afraid
the brief, sharp cries will reconcile them to the moment
when they fall away again. So they rub against each other,
their mouths are dry, then wet, then dry.
They feel themselves at the center of a powerful
and baffled will. They feel
they are almost an animal,
washed up on the shore of a world—
or huddled against the gate of a garden—
to which they can't admit they can never be admitted.

# GARY MIRANDA

## 1979

In his poems, Gary Miranda possesses a quality rare in contemporary art because still rarer in our actual lives: the quality of *thoughtfulness*—what Buddhists (I think) mean by *attentiveness*, which I shall define as the fullest attention given to the least of things, both visible and invisible. He says in one poem, "All things are near"—and this nearness of all things arises directly from Miranda's thoughtfulness about them. One lovely consequence is that, while nothing confuses us, everything enchants us. His art displays emotional courage.

—Donald Sheehan

# Third Elegy

It's one thing to write love poems. Another, though,
to deal with that river-god of the blood: hidden, guilty.
Even the girl, who thinks she knows her young lover,
even she isn't close enough for him to tell
how this lord of lust—in the lonely times
before she knew him, before she eased him, almost
before she seemed possible—would lift up his godhead,
wet with the unknowable, and churn the night
to an endless riot. Such a Neptune in the blood,
with his three-pronged weapon! Such a dark wind
in the chest out of that twisted conch! Listen:
the night is becoming a cave, emptying itself.

Stars, perhaps it's from you that the lover's desire
for the face of his loved one grows; perhaps he
responds to her pure look because he remembers yours.
But it wasn't you, and it wasn't his mother,
who arched his brows into that look of readiness.
It wasn't your mouth, girl—though you hold him—
it wasn't yours that made his own mouth curve
with new ripeness. Do you really think
that your gentle arrival could shatter him so—
you, who move with the softness of a morning breeze?
True, you surprised his heart. But older fears
swept in when your touch startled him. Call him:
you can't distract him completely from those dark
associations. He tries, and he does escape them,
and, relieved, he makes your deepest self his home,
enters, and decides to begin himself new there.
But when did he ever begin himself really?

Mother, *you* made him once, tiny; you began him;
he was new with you. You shaped a friendly world
for his new eyes, shutting the strange one out.
But where did they go—those years when your slight frame
was enough to eclipse a whole world of chaos?
You protected him from so much: at night
you made the threatening bedroom safe; your caring
filled up the space of his night, and made it human.
You placed the nightlight not in the darkness,
but in your closer presence, and it shone like a friend.
There wasn't a creak you couldn't explain away
with a smile—almost as though you expected the floor
to behave that way. And he listened, and it soothed him.
You accomplished so much, so gently, just by rising
and coming to him. His tall, shrouded fate
retreated behind the dresser; his unruly future,
disgruntled, adjusted itself to the folds of the curtain.

And he himself, as he lay there comforted,
drowsily mixing the sweet taste of your presence
with the first taste of sleep, *seemed*
to be well-protected. But *inside*—who, there,
could hold back or channel the flood of his origin?
For he had no sense of fear, asleep.
Sleeping, dreaming, in a kind of fever,
how he wandered off. He—innocent, shy—
how tangled he became in the clinging weeds
of his inner self, already thick with twisted designs,
with clutching undergrowth, with the shapes
of prowling animals. How he surrendered to,
how he loved it! Loved his inner world,
his wilderness within, that primitive jungle inside
where his heart, shimmering green, stood

amid speechless debris. Loved! Passed through it
and, following his roots, arrived at the violent
source where his own birth was already irrelevant.

Descended with love into the older blood,
the ravines where monsters waited, still gorged
with his forefathers. And every monster recognized
him, winked at him, knew. Yes, Horror itself
smiled at him. You've seldom smiled so tenderly, Mother.
And how could he not love it, if it smiled at him!
Before he loved *you* he loved it: even while
you carried him in your womb it was there,
dissolved in the water that cushions the seed.

Look, we don't love, like the flowers, from a single
season. When we love, a sap that has flowed
for countless ages stirs up in our arms. Yes,
girl—*this*: that we've loved *within* ourselves,
not one, not someone we're about to meet,
but the numberless comings-into-being;
not one child only, but all the fathers
who live in our depths like crumbled mountains,
but the parched riverbeds of previous mothers,
but the whole soundless landscape of destiny,
cloudy or cloudless—*this*, girl, was here before you.

And you yourself—how could you know
what an ancient past you awoke in your lover?
What emotions flared up from beings no longer here!
What women inside him hated you! What sinister
men you aroused in his young veins! Dead children
stretched out their hands to you... Oh
gently, gently, show him the steady love

in a daily task, attract him toward the garden,
make him a gift of the irresistible nights....

Hold him...back.

# Witnessing

*—for Patty*

Beneath leaves of a plant that's named for milk,
that bleeds milk, we search for chrysalides—
things that I've never seen, but whose name I like.
And I think, as I look, of all the things

you've taught me to name—larkspur, loose-
strife, sea lavender, plants called hens
and chickens, butter and eggs, your eyes
bright with such knowledge, as solid as nouns.

Just so, you tell me now of creatures
who choose the underbelly of these leaves to make
wombs of, studded with gold, from which emerge
monarchs that range the length of the Atlantic

in hordes—one more fact I must have missed
by skipping the fourth grade. And when, today,
we find no trace of anything resembling this
miracle you mention, and I'm about to say

you made it up, you bend down, break a pod,
and blow unlikely butterflies in the sky's face
not black and orange like monarchs, but cloud-
thought white, or like the way I mark my place

when I read your eyes, which, witnessing, claim:
*This is the world. Try to learn its name.*

# Like Snow

Some people would remember iron
railings, the color of buildings,
how a dog circled three times
before settling in—novelists,
certainly, or just good talkers.

Most of us take only the light
from a place, and translate even that
into the way our spirits shape
the light. We flash into knowledge,
which, if we ignore it, will not forgive us.

Objects can survive fine on their own,
but the feel for how this face, that
window, falls upon the momentary
way we hold ourselves could easily
get lost, and who would find it?

Such loss, if lived with, stiffens
into pain; it stands up, starched
and handsome, ready to please the neighbors.
We find ourselves forgetting dreams, whole
days, the last time we were honest;

we ask ourselves: say something
in childhood, and feel only the weight
of what that means brush against
our face like snow. "Like snow,"
we say, not even coming close.

# Triptych

*—for Marianne Vonzweck*

## 1. *Icarus*

You never hear about my mother, though that sun,
imploding its brilliant exigencies, bore
a striking resemblance, up close. My father
should have warned me—though perhaps I just
wasn't listening or had no experience
to tune my ear to his meaning. I could tell
you about rage, now: archipelagoes of red
detonating in some liquid, but not quite
mixing; aloft on its wings, the mind remarking
even in its terror: Lovely...lovely! Perhaps
I fell because I wanted to tell my brother
the sea what it was like up there, or warn him,
in terms he might understand, to escape.

Idling in the blue air, the left wing of my
silence tilted toward home, a nervous
tic I hoped to correct with practice. Wax
might really have worked had that breast
practiced a little self-control, not blazed so
with passion, incestuous. Worn down by the sea,
no sibling of mine as it turns out, these
feathers grow incongruous, hardly suffice
as fins, resemble—if anything—the nubbins
of a three-month fetus. Wiser now, I learn
to use what I have, shuffling toward shore.
Flying is for birds. Given a second
choice, I decide to be born.

## 2. *Orpheus*

Darkness bloomed, and in that space
which was the shape, still, of the flower,
light declared its name—a sound I knew.
But I knew too the illusion of trust
that touches all we can name by language,
calling the sky "a grey slate" or clouds
"the color of erasure." How much we trust
depends on what's at stake in my case,
love, I thought, though I was mistaken.
Trees understand the word for "sky,"
but not for "leaf," as if the whole of life
were learning to know the enemy—that is,
the one from whom you need love the most.

The importance of what we want is clear,
however inaccurate. The sound of it
follows us at distances too close
to question, like the sound of a dripping
faucet you hear—listen for, rather—when
the faucet is not dripping: a kind
of silence, spliced; or the way an eye
fixes for a moment a star, any star,
then loses it again. "Gun" will never do
for that object, held to the back of your head.
Call it "history." You will learn to forgive it.
You turn around to face your first love,
Darkness, gone. And you hold your own.

## 3. *Sisyphus*

All things are near, imagining. The words
of sages, or even of damn good poets, seem
easy enough once they're out there, shimmering.
If I could, I would lift this stone like a crust
in the wind and wait for the gull of time
to dive, or spin it, light as vowels in the mouths
of infants, who choke on the coarse consonants.
I would strike an armistice with stone, saying:
your metaphors hold, they last—the child
against the radiator its head, the drunk
into the hard bench of winter, heart in the rib
cage, tongue in the teeth. This stone is a moon
against which the wolf of my one life howls.

Courage is not inexhaustible. It gets beaten
down to a fine edge of sadness, like that slice
of horizon crushed between earth and sky.
Or like an old woman who sits and darns,
replacing the essence of socks with the dark
thread of her own death, reducing all clothes
to the negative of clothes. But look: how
she makes the tiny point turn needle again,
the way a god might push a star clear through
from the other side. Such motion precludes meaning,
or else defines it. I have a gift for making truth
irrelevant. Behind my eyes, like a lost shoulder
of the sea, the moon of my next self rises.

# Listeners at the Breathing Place

*"The seal hunters sometimes call themselves
listeners at the breathing places."*
—from *Eskimo Prints*, by James Houston

The air says what it means, regardless of what
we want it to say. It holds our breath. Conundrums
tumble like seals. We listen. We catch one,
if we are lucky, the way a camera catches the gallop
of horses, their legs in positions we would never imagine.

Van Gogh knew. There is something to be said
for the word's inadequacies, the swirls of light
and movement which will always escape, astound us.
Rain on water, a lover's turning to go. Those places
breathe too, saying: "Be brave, believe in us."

In the end, we will lay down our words and embrace
the air that shapes them here, just as, at the peak
of loving, a cry shakes the candle's aureola in a room
too small for all this, and the body for now needs
to be held, to be held back, from that blinding other.

# WILLIAM MATTHEWS

## 1980

In his poems, William Matthews touches that spring of Western lyricism that Frost himself touched: classical Latin. But where Frost fashioned an apparent *rural* simplicity (as did Horace), Matthews establishes a genuine *urban* complexity—not the city of headlines but (again, Horace) the city of shrewdness and bravery, a city of studied casualness and genuine longing. Thus he brings to his poems a voice made urbane and musical, in the ways Frost's great poems were: a voice that makes our terror comprehensible by unveiling the underlying comedy.

—Donald Sheehan

# On the Porch at the Frost Place,
# Franconia, NH

*—for Stanley Plumly*

So here the great man stood,
fermenting malice and poems
we have to be nearly as fierce
against ourselves as he
not to misread by their disguises.
Blue in dawn haze, the tamarack
across the road is new since Frost
and thirty feet tall already.
No doubt he liked to scorch off
morning fog by simply staring through it
long enough so that what he saw
grew visible. "Watching the dragon
come out of the Notch," his children
used to call it. And no wonder
he chose a climate whose winter
and house whose isolation could be
stern enough to his wrath and pity
as to make them seem survival skills
he'd learned on the job, farming
fifty acres of pasture and woods.
For cash crops he had sweat and doubt
and moralizing rage, those staples
of the barter system. And these swift
and aching summers, like the blackberries
I've been poaching down the road
from the house where no one's home—
acid at first and each little globe
of the berry too taut and distinct
from the others, then they swell to hold

the riot of their juices and briefly
the fat berries are perfected to my taste,
and then they begin to leak and blob
and under their crescendo of sugar
I can taste how they make it through winter....
By the time I'm back from a last,
six-berry raid, it's almost dusk,
and more and more mosquitoes
will race around my ear their tiny engines,
the speedboats of the insect world.
I won't be longer on the porch
than it takes to look out once
and see what I've taught myself
in two months here to discern:
night restoring its opacities,
though for an instant as intense
and evanescent as waking from a dream
of eating blackberries and almost
being able to remember it, I think
I see the parts—haze, dusk, light
broken into grains, fatigue,
the mineral dark of the White Mountains,
the wavering shadows steadying themselves—
separate, then joined, then seamless:
the way, in fact, Frost's great poems,
like all great poems, conceal
what they merely know, to be
predicaments. However long
it took to watch what I thought
I saw, it was dark when I was done,
everywhere and on the porch,
and since nothing stopped
my sight, I let it go.

# Civilization and Its Discontents

*Integration in, or adaptation to, a human community appears as a scarcely avoidable condition which must be fulfilled before [our] aim of happiness can be achieved. If it could be done without that condition, it would perhaps be preferable.* —Freud

How much of the great poetry
of solitude in the woods is one
long cadenza on the sadness

of civilization, and how much
thought on beaches, between drowsing
and sleep, along the borders,

between one place and another,
as if such poise were home to us?
On the far side of these woods, stew,

gelatinous from cracked lamb shanks,
is being ladled into bowls, and
a family scuffs its chairs close

to an inherited table.
Maybe there's wine, maybe not. We don't
know because our thoughts are with

the great sad soul in the woods again.
We suppose that even now
some poignant speck of litter

borne by the river of psychic murmur
has been grafted by the brooding soul
to a beloved piece of music,

and that from the general plaint
a shape is about to be made, though
maybe not: we can't see into

the soul the way we can into
that cottage where now they're done with food
until next meal. Here's what I think:

the soul in the woods is not alone.
All he came there to leave behind
is in him, like a garrison

in a conquered city. When he goes
back to it, and goes gratefully
because it's nearly time for dinner,

he will be entering himself,
though when he faced the woods,
from the road, that's what he thought then, too.

# Loyal

They gave him an overdose
of anesthetic, and its fog
shut down his heart in seconds.
I tried to hold him, but he was
somewhere else. For so much of love
one of the principals is missing,
it's no wonder we confuse love
with longing. Oh I was thick
with both. I wanted my dog
to live forever and while I was
working on impossibilities
I wanted to live forever, too.
I wanted company and to be alone.
I wanted to know how they trash
a stiff ninety-five-pound dog
and I paid them to do it
and not tell me. What else?
I wanted a letter of apology
delivered by decrepit hand,
by someone shattered for each time
I'd had to eat pure pain. I wanted
to weep, not "like a baby,"
in gulps and breath-stretching
howls, but steadily, like an adult,
according to the fiction
that there is work to be done,
and almost inconsolably.

# Inspiration

Rumpled, torpid, bored, too tasteful to rhyme
"lethargy" with "laundry," or too lazy,
I'll not spend my afternoon at the desk
cunningly weaving subjunctives and lithe
skeins of barbed colloquial wire. Today

I loathe poetry. I hate the clotted,
dicty poems of the great modernists,
disdainful of their truant audience,
and I hate also proletarian
poetry, with its dutiful rancors

and sing-along certainties. I hate
poetry readings and the dreaded verb
"to share." Let me share this knife with your throat,
suggested Mack. Today I'm a gnarl, a knot,
a burl. I'm furled in on myself and won't

be opened. I'm the bad mood if you try
to cheer me out of I'll smack you. Impasse
is where I come to escape from. It takes
a deep belief in one's own ignorance;
it takes, I tell you, desperate measures.

# My Father's Body

First they take it away,
for now the body belongs to the state.
Then they open it
to see what may have killed it,
and the body had arteriosclerosis
in its heart, for this was an inside job.
Now someone must identify the body
so that the state may have a name
for what it will give away,
and the funeral people come in a stark car
shaped like a coffin with a hood
and take the body away,
for now it belongs to the funeral people
and the body's family buys it back,
though it lies in a box at the crematorium
while the mourners travel and convene.
Then they bring the body to the chapel, as they call it,
of the crematorium, and the body lies in its box
while the mourners enter and sit
and stare at the box, for the box
lies on a pedestal where the altar would be
if this were a chapel.
A rectangular frame with curtains at the sides
rises from the pedestal,
so that the box seems to fill a small stage,
and the stage gives off the familiar
illusion of being a box with one wall torn away
so that we may see into it,
but it's filled with a box we can't see into.
There's music on tape and a man in a robe
speaks for a while and I speak

for a while and then there's a prayer
and then we mourners can hear the whir
of a small motor and curtains slide
across the stage. At least for today,
I think, this is the stage that all the world is,
and another motor hums on
and we mourners realize that behind
the curtains the body is being lowered,
not like Don Giovanni to the flames
but without flourish or song
or the comforts of elaborate plot,
to the basement of the crematorium,
to the mercies of the gas jets
and the balm of the conveyer belt.
The ashes will be scattered,
says a hushed man in a mute suit,
in the Garden of Remembrance,
which is out back.
And what's left of a mild, democratic man
will sift in a heap with the residue of others,
for now they all belong to time.

# The Rented House in Maine

At dawn, the liquid clatter of rain
pocks the bay and stutters on the roof.
Even when it's this gray, the first slant light
predicts across the rug gaunt shadows
of the generic paper birds
my landlord's pasted to the eastern wall,

all glass, to fend specific birds
from bonking themselves dull or worse
against the bright blare of false sky.
From the bay the house must look
like a grade-school homeroom gussied up
for parents' night. I like to build

a small fire first thing in the morning,
drink some coffee, drive to town,
buy the *Times*, drive back to embers
the color of canned tomato soup
(made not with water but with milk).
In this house I fell—no hurled myself—

in love, and elsewhere, day by day,
it didn't last. Tethered to lobster traps,
buoys wobble on the bay. On the slithering
surface of the water, the rain seems
to explode—chill shrapnel, and I look
away. Ember and cool coffee. Matter,

energy, the speed of light: the universe
can be explained by an equation. Everything
that goes from one side of the equal sign

is exactly replaced from the other; i.e.,
nothing much happens at a speed so fast
we scarcely notice it, but so steadily

the math always checks out. This is thought
as I know and love it. Why did that marriage
fail? I know the reasons and count the ways.
The clouds with squalls in their cheeks,
like chaws or tongues, have broken up.
The fire is down, the coffee cold, the sun is up.

# MARY JO SALTER

## 1981

In her poems, Mary Jo Salter exhibits what most delights us about the best poems of Wallace Stevens: elegant and graceful joy in the everyday things of the world. But Salter creates poems without the least touch of Stevens's self-absorbed philosophizing. Instead, she gives us emotionally honest, heartbreaking clarity, and the most straightforward of narrative lines. The great Roman lyric poet Horace asks, *damnosa quid non imminuit dies?* Poet David Ferry translates: "What is there that has been left unruined?" Mary Jo Salter's poems respond beautifully to the endless desolations; what is unruined is this capacity for graceful joy.

—Donald Sheehan

# The Seven Weepers

The tines of his comb were splitting into finer
brittle strands, like hair, but his own hair—
deader than a corpse's, which can lengthen
in the sweet cool of the coffin—had stopped growing.
Screws unscrewed themselves from wooden boxes
where the stone-dry food was kept. Matches ignited
magically in air, as they fell to earth.
And who would believe it? When he took his pen
to paper, to record the temperature—
a hundred fifty-seven in the sun,
in the shade a hundred thirty-two—the ink
dried at the nib; the lead dropped whole from pencils.
What he had wanted was to draw a line
on the map from Adelaide into the heart
of the outback, where he'd willed a vast Australian
sea like the Caspian. But water holes
of a single shrinking creek were all they'd found,
like the globules of a burst thermometer.

Worst, he thought, was how the rising moon
offered no respite—so blinding that the black
swans that flew across its surface seemed
charred in the passage. Mostly, nothing moved
but ants and lizards. He who had fought
with Wellington against the French, who quelled
riots in Ireland, and headed a convict guard
all the way to the wrong end of the world,
where summer raged in January, now
had loitered with his men and bulls and horses
by a nameless pool, with debilitating wisdom,
six months for a drop of rain. In July it came.

And watered them enough to drag themselves
safely for a while across the blank
he named the Stony Desert, with a compass
that couldn't tell them when they should turn back
from infernal sandhills, burnished red, so hard
the horses left no track, as in a dream.
Twice they retrenched and shifted course when hope
of water dried up, shallow and absurd:
a pigeon diving steeply into shadow
that might be mud but wasn't; a clump of bush.
In November a seagull, five hundred miles from sea,
led them to a salt lake, purplish blue,
the color of Heaven.

        What then was this scene
of misery they'd stumbled on? Years later
in England, nearly blind, Charles Sturt would wake
some mornings to that sight of seven naked
black men in a circle by the lake,
wailing and weeping. So profligate! he thought,
spending their grief like that. Who knew
when it would rain again, or if the sun
would bake away this pond of indigo
to nothing? Fools. Better save your tears.

Some in his group knew tribal words, and tried them.
What was the matter? A death? But all the words
were wrong, and the seven weepers seemed
as if they'd long forgotten what it meant
to have an answer. Inconsolable
is all they were. —Somewhere beyond the terror
he'd caused once, early on, in native eyes,
when he'd come bounding forward on his horse.
It wasn't the horse, exactly, but himself

dismounting from it: apparently they'd thought
white man and horse were one, a sort of Centaur.

And yet there were no Centaurs, no such creatures
ever in their heads: the thought now struck him
with the beating of the sun (or so the tale
would go if one retold it as one chose,
too far from 1845 to say
what any of them were) that these were men
wholly unlike himself. What songs they chanted
into the air could only evaporate,
though their chimeras—like the man-sized snake
and the red, preposterous kangaroo—were real.
*Hath the rain a father? Or who hath begotten*
*The drops of dew?* That voice, which thundered now
in the groping cloud of dust that was his mind—
where had it come from?—was of course the voice
of God in the whirlwind, chastising his servant.
And hadn't Job lost seven sons? What help
that fact was to him, he could hardly say,
but he stood there wrapped in silence while the naked
sinners wept, until he could remember
that Job had sat for seven days in silence
before he spoke.

          He didn't have a week
to wait for them; his handkerchief was a rag.
Charles Sturt, whose nation soon would drape its flag
over the weepers' country like a shroud,
reached from his Christian soul and in the heat
uselessly, kindly, gave them his overcoat.

# CLEOPATRA MATHIS

## 1982

In her poems, Cleopatra Mathis exhibits an emotional honesty, in that the more complex the emotion becomes, the clearer her poems become. The lyric impulse seems somehow brighter as the danger of emotional meltdown draws nearer. I want to bring forth Medea—not the Medea of the Greek Euripedes but the Medea of the Roman Seneca: that pure state of mind rushing far past every consolation—even the last consolation of self-annihilation—to where our deepest love takes firmest root, a place of extraordinary tenderness. Cleopatra Mathis's poetry faces the *mystery* of emotional life.

—Donald Sheehan

# What Disappears

in Louisiana: start with a name,
birthright, stolen away
with my father's bus ride

to Texas and who-knows-where.
He took the Cherokee part of me,
left the Greek I traded

for a kind of English I'd later
slough off in shame. The color of skin
divided the town, kept me

from certain faces, the same ones
who left us peaches or purple-hull peas
before dawn. Daylight swallowed them up,

swallowed the cheap talk, childhood
with its hand-me-down dresses.
Years went their way, stripping

my brother's small esteem, that smile of his,
long before the night he vanished
from my mother's house. What disappears

is his body, sunk in the puzzle of the bayou.
I took myself out of that swamp,
took eighteen years, came back

with love's intention. How can a place
be made for losing? Right out of my pocket,
the hair clip made of gold

from my good life, the leather purse
cradled on my lap. I won't turn my back
on my baby, my perfect blond boy

who's nine and wants to shake me off.
I hover while he's sleeping in my old bed.
I'm out on the porch, I'm watching.

# What to Tip the Boatman?

Delicate—the way at three she touched
her hands tip to tip, each finger a rib
framing the tepee of her hands.
So tentative that joining, taking
tender hold of her body, as if the ballast
of her selfhood rested there. Already
she could thread tiny beads through the eye
and onto string, correctly placing
each letter of her name, sorting
thin black lines to make an alphabet,
the needle just so in her little hand.
She loved that necklace less
than cat's cradle, a game to weave
the strand through forefinger, ringfinger, pinkie.
She could lace a basket, a boat
that could even carry water. *What to tip
the boatman?* I asked, trying to amuse her
with church and steeple turned to my empty palm.
Naptime, she'd lie there making shapes
above her, signing the air.

Later I saw the light touch in those twinned
fingertips had become her way
of holding still, keeping balance.
She had reached home before I did, finding
no mother at the bus stop, and entered
the silenced house for the first time alone.
Ancient, venerable, the whole place
waited, a relative with smells and creaks
she hesitated to greet. When I found her
she had made her way to the formal great room,

polite center of the hectic house where even
the clock's old thud gave back the heart
of simple waiting. Good guest, a shadow
on the rose Victorian settee, she sat,
her hands precise before her, an offering.

# Solstice

### 1.

The child, thirteen, pushing away
the clip that tamed her hair.
The child with a pistol against her ear.
In the great life of things, a small noise
against the noise of spring. So small,
the mother downstairs only heard
the sound of something falling.

### 2.

She went, young enough to believe
nothingness is an empty field—
so many blackbirds out there you couldn't see,
wings with their red and yellow bars, the one
clear note coming from somewhere, a nest
to settle in. Where she fell, a world
would rise to hold her.
Isn't that what the story teaches?

### 3.

They stumble in the yard: the parents
leading all the classmates
stunned around them. Just beyond the funeral
heat, a meadow burns in the glare,
the new hay whitens.
Every parent invents a story.

4.

No one knew she wanted the dark, this girl
whispering into a book—
already a woman's tongue, an eye.
A last shake of her hair, and another world
took her words, the ground opened
for her bones. She's under the nursery-grown
tree's accomplished shape, a small fact

fixed between the pine and lilac.
She was young enough to want a home down there.
And the ghost you've heard for months now,
that's what failure sounds like:
explaining and explaining.

# Noon

1.

What adolescent can bear her mother?
Her words, her touch. The baby
who clung to my ample thigh
veers away, whips her horse
to go faster. She's testing
this gelding; she will have him
charging through the afternoon—reckless will
aiming for that surge
in the chest, the swallow of romantic dark.

2.

Something's wrong. The day's brilliance
shakes the horse. His eyes whiten,
he throws his head—some command
bears down from the heaven
of sun-eaten blue. Circling, circling,
the girl uses what she knows:
leg grip, seat, the danger
in showing the horse her fear.
*I can't stop him*, she says
as they bolt past. The field's sod rips
and heaves, black ruts
open for the stumble.

All I can think is how calm she is,
caught in a fury that promises
to send her flying. Now she's forward

in the saddle, willing to go
with what's been given. Flushed, steady,
her hands stay quiet, cupping the reins
as she's been taught.

# Search

An itch I couldn't get to
lived in my eyes. I scratched,
they burned. No make-up, no balm,
I clutched the wheel, I drove
through the rural wash of snow and salt
to the hospital. The enemy's address

was somewhere in her head. I drove
in and out of blackness, smelled the shit
on the farmer's road. My eyes swelled to slits,
narrowed, hardened. Yes, I'd be a bird of prey,
I'd go after the dark.
                              Led to her,
I took her face in my hands, peered
as if to find the small child she'd been,
the infant, the embryo. I wanted her
so far back she'd disappear inside me.

I couldn't find the way in. I couldn't see
into her face, which had become like clay
shaped by pills and needles into no look at all.
Nothing but the inward
listening to the god of the backwards clock.

# The Return

You magic thing, you brother,
erupting from underneath,
swallowing up whatever you wish.
Not enough to own everything below
this ground I govern, no,
you with your kingdom of rocks
took my one uncut jewel.
You wanted something new
turning this way and that on your throne
down there. Now she's eaten the earth's seeds,
you have to give her up. She'll be back,
but never with that innocence
you wanted.

We'll both have her, but it's nothing
more than a bargain she's bound to keep.
She's carved a self now—not for you
or me. Look how carefully,
gleaming in the light,
she rows herself out.

# Under Moose Mountain

1.

I spoke to the house: I am leaving you
I said. A house is not the world,
though it may serve as body. The house
is not flesh, though it held us
sometimes like a fist, sometimes
blowing into an ear with its silks
of light and air. Ghosts, we said at first,
catching the whisper as it flew past,
settling in the door frame, crooked
but holding everything up. The first year
I couldn't bear that hint of a voice
just over my shoulder. It sent me out
past the driveway into the woods,
the noisy layers of night I preferred
to fires in every room, the history
of breathing and dying an old house knows

—the way it knows children, and calls them,
answers the fact of their loneliness
with its own creaking as the child lies
watching in the night. Even I learned
to take that comfort, first a place
to house my fear, later a precious thing
I'd trade for my daughter's health.
That old sad note in her
still plays, echoing, lasting
like the row of maples dying on ledge
these last hundred years. What gets added

is her childhood, a little story
that came out right.

I walk through rooms, and this time
the dark is just an incidental thing,
a chipped bowl, a cradle in the corner,
part of what's been lived. Fifteen years
of stumbling over the uneven floors, random
nails appearing overnight on the scarred
pine boards, dependable as the groaning
farm truck at dawn, its empty bed
sounding in the loose windows. My footfall
rattles the teacups under glass,
every sound and slant of light tracing
back to the beginning, when the cabinet
was built into the wall. Where the sun
has always found it, sweeping over
the forked road, past the oak cradling
a fallen birch in the old V of its trunk,
past my thick work of summer flowers
in the bed I tamed from a slag pit,
lugging rocks away
to dig that front border deep enough
to sustain anything I planted.


2.


My daughter packs up the room I learned
to dread in the pitch-dark of its map.
Mild now in the afternoon,
it's stripped to the walls, the ceiling
painted once again. All winter,

moisture from the humidifier's drip
rose to sweat away the new white coat
from the layer of panicked scrawl, red
shoved into the black she fought
with a blade that scarred more than wood.
The revelation

somehow pleases her: a picked lock.
*When you were sick*: my smoothed voice
casual, turned away, not showing the girl
my grief for a place I want now to redeem,
not abandon. Naked, pale,
it stands empty, four walls and a floor
giving back the hollow of our voices.

Finished, she lets the silence
spin around her—nothing
as she pauses at the top of her stair,
a world surveyed one last time,
then clatters down. We quit her childhood,
we quit the house, an old relative
who holds the key to a few family years,
the real story living in that body
we know we won't see again. In this way
we all change places, she the mother
to the girl, and I—who will I be
when I finish all this sweeping and scrubbing,
part of me leaving,
walking out, locking the door?

# DENIS JOHNSON

## 1983

I n his poems, Denis Johnson brings the novelist's joy in the grittiest specificities to a place where lyric patterning is loved for its own beautiful sake: the vivid specificities of actual places and real personalities. In his lyric patterning Denis Johnson accomplishes what every poet since the ancient poet Horace has wanted to accomplish: the registering of a literary intelligence in which the real world actually is seen and heard and tasted. Denis Johnson's poems make us see again that present reality always contains the deepest aliveness imaginable. And his poems sing this aliveness.

—Donald Sheehan

# The Rockefeller Collection of Primitive Art

Softer my neighbor rocks his lover through the human night,
softly and softly, so as not to tell the walls,
the walls the friends of the spinster. But I'm only a spinster,
I'm not a virgin. I have made love. I have known desire.

I followed desire through the museums.
We seemed to float along sculptures,
along the clicking ascent
of numerals in the guards' hands. Brave works
by great masters were all around us.

And then we came out of a tunnel into one of those restaurants
where the natural light was so unnatural
as to make heavenly even our fingernails and each radish.
I saw everyone's skull beneath the skin,
I saw sorrow painting its way out of the faces,
someone was telling a lie and I could taste it,
and I heard the criminal tear-fall,
saw the dog
who dances with his shirt rolled up to his nipples,
the spider...

Why are their mouths small tight circles,
the figures of Africa, New Guinea, New Zealand,
why are their mouths astonished kisses beneath drugged eyes,
why is the eye of the cantaloup expressionless
but its skin rippling with terror,
and out beyond Coney Island in the breathless waste
of Atlanta, why
does the water move when it is already there?

My neighbor's bedsprings struggle
—soon she will begin to scream—

I think of them always
travelling through space,
riding their bed so
softly it staves the world through the air
of my room—it is their right,
because we freely admit how powerful the sight is,
we say that eyes stab and glances rake,
but it is not the sight
that lets us taste the salt on someone's shoulder in the night,
the musk of fear in the morning,
the savor of falling in the falling
elevators in the buildings of rock,
it is the dark that lets us it is the dark. If
I can imagine them then
why can't I imagine this?

# The Monk's Insomnia

The monastery is quiet. Seconal
drifts down upon it from the moon.
I can see the lights
of the city I came from,
can remember how a boy sets out
like something thrown from the furnace
of a star. In the conflagration of memory
my people sit on green benches in the park,
terrified, evil, broken by love—
to set with them inside that invisible fire
of hours day after day while the shadow of the milk
billboard crawled across the street
seemed impossible, but how
was it different from here,
where they have one day they play over
and over as if they think
it is our favorite, and we stay
for our natural lives,
a phrase that conjures up the sun's
dark ash adrift after ten billion years
of unconsolable burning? Brother Thomas's
schoolgirl obsession with the cheap
doings of TV starlets breaks
everybody's heart, and the yellow sap
of one particular race of cactus grows
tragic for the fascination in which
it imprisons Brother Toby—I can't witness
his slavering and relating how it can be changed
into some unprecedented kind of plastic—
and the monastery refuses
to say where it is taking us. At night

we hear the trainers from the base
down there, and see them blotting out the stars,
and I stand on the hill and listen, bone-white with desire.
It was love that set me on the journey,
love that called me home. But it's the terror
of being just one person—one chance, one set of days—
that keeps me absolutely still tonight and makes me listen
intently to those young men above us
flying in their airplanes in the dark.

# SHEROD SANTOS

## 1984

I n his poems, Sherod Santos exhibits an engaging sensi-
bility once perfectly expressed by a character in a story
by J. D. Salinger, who said: "I suspect myself of being a
paranoid in reverse, that the whole world is conspiring to
make me happy." As a result, Santos's poems are packed with
people—some grieving, others thick with deception, all of
them heartbreaking—people whom the poet persuades us to
love not because they're beautiful but because they're so
amazingly alive. His poems are like that moment in the
Eastern Orthodox liturgical year, toward dawn on Easter
Sunday, after everyone has gone through the long, terrible
night of Christ's death, when all the worshipers cry out
together in joy: Christ has risen! Truly He has risen!

—Donald Sheehan

# The Conversation

It's odd because, beyond that day, there's not
Much else he remembers about the summer
He spent near Bridal Falls while she went home
To California to visit with some friends.
They'd been married four or five years by then,
And this, they realized, was the longest
They'd ever been separated, a fact that shadowed
Their conversation in the days before they left.
"Do we love each other less?" she'd asked,
One morning over coffee, and by way
Of illustration she had summoned that squat
Misshapen form the ancients believed
Eros degraded into as we age. "Does this
Mean that we are turning into *that*?"
                                        At first
He thought this is one of those things that lovers
Talk about in order to have them talked away,
The words themselves a kind of talisman
Against the very thing they named; but then
She started to reach across the breakfast table
To take his hand, and he could see in the way
Some unchecked reflex drew it back that this
Was something she hadn't named; and now
That it was there, now that it had hunkered down
Between them, then no words no matter how
Sincere would ever completely dispel its fear.

But memories, like dreams, are rarely self-
Contained, and he recalls all that as context for
The memory of what followed. Mid-August.
High range. Loose stands of aspen on the lower

Slopes. Scattered cabins along a county road
And a turn-of-the-century pinewood lodge
Whose out-buildings were converted into quarters
For the seasonal staff and guides. One night
Following a round of cards in the dining hall,
He wandered back to his cabin late and thought
To write her a letter. The wind wasn't up yet,
A broad wadeable trout stream was just
Audible at the willow bend, and farther still,
A half-hour walk up a logging road, a series
Of beautiful, precipitous falls.

                                    He'd paused
To smoke a cigarette at the willow bend,
And striking a match had startled a rummaging
Groundhog from a mess of scrub oak and sage.
He felt it first brush against his leg, then heard
Its padded footfalls as it sidled into the open
Where, circumspect and nosing the air,
It curled around in the middle of the road
To clean its iridescent fur in the scumbling
Half-light of a risen moon. Fattened
On field mice, self-content, wholly at home
In the gathering fullness of early summer,
It squired above its small domain,
Its wedge-shaped head sliding in one long
Liquid arc from side to side, a kind of casual
Going over of everything there around it,
Everything quickened by summer dust.

And then he thought it settled its leveling
Gaze on him. He tried to imagine what it was
It saw. Some vague nocturnal shape?
An appalling otherness intruding on
The marked-out limits of its ground? Whatever

It was, what he saw looking back at him
Was a figure of that thing she'd feared,
The unwinged creature of their desire annealed
And toughened over, glutted somehow,
The dull, lumpish animal of it slaked,
Complacent, overfilled, and for all of that
Imperious in the dry-eyed prospect
Of its nature.
                    The trout stream ran, or seems
To run, somewhere under that memory,
The rhythm of it emptying into the confusion
Of the days to come: the maddened flurry
Of telephone calls, the tears, reproaches,
Their trips cut short, a flood of apologies
And regrets until they couldn't really say
What happened to them. Like all such fears,
Throughout the intervening years this one
Rose and disappeared so often that they'd come
To feel that it was a kind of longing too,
A part of them that wants as well,
That makes their separate presence felt
In ways that cause the heart to fly up into
The chest, as his does now, twenty years later,
Lying there beside her while she falls asleep,
Her hair, like his, declining into gray,
Her body, like his, heavier and more familiar,
Her face, like his, overlaid with the spider trace
Of middle age. But struggle as he will
To understand, he cannot connect his own death
To the purblind terror that's come over him.

# Dairy Cows at Crawford Farm

*Islandmagee, County Antrim*

Still road-weary but quite warmly stowed
Beneath a goose-down duvet in the B&B,
I awaken to a lowing stream of cows
Flooding the field behind a milking barn,

A scene that seems to have followed me here
From childhood, the traced illustrations
Of a nursery rhyme (their watercolors not even
Thought of once in over thirty-five years),

Or a Sunday's hour-long lesson on a notion
That surely eluded me then, *the peace*
*Which passeth understanding.* So framed,
The mind's rumination deepens like a dream,

And like a dream from which the mind's eye
Culls, not the particulars of a landscape
(Withheld, in any case, as sun and mist
Alike lift off the inwardly greening hills)

But the mute disbursements of an emotion
That's composed, in part, of earth and air,
So too my window opens on a feeling
I can't separate from those dozen or more

Milk cows milling about the grasslands
Of the Crawford's farm. It follows then
That the mind takes pleasure in puzzling out
How something within their cumbered

Motions through the morning air recalls
That instinct pastured where the slow, pacific
Form thought takes is given time to reflect
On thought: thought thinking thought,

And the once unthinkable end of thought,
*Whereof one cannot speak, thereof one must be silent.*
So wherever they go, alone or at times
Beside themselves wading the mud lanes

Out from the dairy, or grazing the sketched in
Grasses by the pond, they move the way
A low-forming storm cloud moves,
Trolling the earth out of which it draws

In the welling concentration of a passing hour
A heaviness it must soon become.
And yet a cow jumped over the moon,
We're told, and what has ever more easily

Slipped the snare of its own burden,
Turned burden, by nature, to beneficence,
Than the plush surprise releasing along
Their bloodstream's course a plenitude spiked,

As Virgil claimed, with salt herb, lotus,
And shrub trefoil. A plenitude which, to temper
That bitterness we drink to warm and clarify
The day, I stream out into a steaming mug

Delivered, like gladness, on a scuffed brass tray.

# A Valley in the Shadow of North Hollywood

As if cued to the first peach prayer-call of sunrise,
The scattered choir of radio alarm clocks
Summon the sleeping body from celestial time
To a work-week morning in the suburbs where,

With a backwoods preacher's broadcast squall,
The day-long labor of a garbage truck begins
Again to dispense with each upended fall
The welling burden of our discontents.

Our first thoughts, then, are of garbage cans
And the human soul, that ancient service
By which the one laid low is taken in hand,
Impelled once more to reclaim its outcast

Station in the home; or, as the case may be,
Unheavened altogether on the paving stones,
A reminder that, no matter how fully a soul
Comes clean, there are certain transgressions

Which still require some harder pardon, some
Suffering we'll manage to overlook when,
For example, cresting the high prospect of an
Overpass, the sun relapses and the addict climbs

Back to the storm pipe he's made his home.
And called to the reckoning of that hour,
Each evening's trail of car lights pours
In slow procession down the valley floor,

Where the underground sprinklers in crowned
Suspiring arcs have left the lawns incensed,
The rinsed curbs blessed by waters to receive
Such pale illumination as one might see,

Or imagine one sees, when a garage door opens
And lo and behold it somehow happens
That a light both inside and out comes on,
And for one brief moment turns everything gold.

# Book of Blessings

The reserved and slightly weary-eyed doctor in the ER who,
Having awakened him late, curled up in a blanket
On the waiting room floor, said two times softly, 'She'll
Be fine now,' that doctor was writ in his Book of Blessings.

As were the windfall apples the horses ate (their trailing
Slobber's acrid stain like the wrack of nature across his hand)
At the Shaker village in Kentucky where his mother had gone
To recover. And the tears of his mother, muffled, exhausted,

Utterly undone by her night-long struggles in the room
Next door, while the boy sat watching on a television screen
The man a following crowd called 'King,' though the crowd
Surrounding did not bow down in the Selma of 1965.

And yet the King's high seeing still gazed beyond the fear
In everyone's eyes to a place made quiet by him in them,
So that the crowd as it passed made a papery sound,
Like the scrape of leaves (or, as the boy now saw it,

Like the theme of leaves) across the threshold that opened
Within him there. That too was writ in his Book of Blessings.
As were the songs he'd committed to memory, the one about
A fast-falling eventide, the one about stardust and a garden wall;

And before that there was learning to read, the alphabet,
Syllable, word and phrase, the vanishing point
Of the period, the tripled period's placid sea...and suspended
Roundly above that sea, the fluent figure of a risen moon,

And the loosed imagining *moon* adds to speech,
The sea change its four letters form in the mind of a boy
Sitting up in bed, until the bed's no longer a bed at all,
But a boat whose filling spinnaker has hauled it out

From a foreign shore overgrown with shadow-shapes
And rustlings. And his penis erect in a dream that boat now
Carries him toward, a dream in which the towering secret
Of his begetting is at last spelled out in the bright pearl-

Droplets of a falling rain, as though the moon were weeping
On the open sea, and the sea were a body it yearned for.
All that was writ in his book as well. All that
And more than he is able to recall tonight, for after

Forty-eight years he has come to find so many erasures
Appear there now, so many passages torn out whole,
While in the Book of Death the pages are already filling up,
And in the Book of Silence, and in the Book of Forgetting.

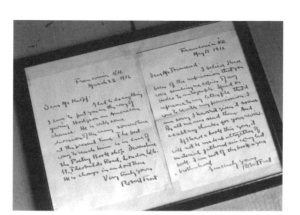

# KATHY FAGAN

## 1985

Kathy Fagan trusts in her poems to a dimension of the lyric that is nearly impossible to manage well: the dimension of speed. Lyrical speed loves straight acceleration, loves the rush to devour the things that can only stay still. Fagan's poems manage lyric acceleration by employing the most astonishing strategy imaginable: she makes speed become an emotional clarification of where we actually are. That is, as she picks up speed in a poem, she gathers in and gives voice to all the emotions that are prompting her to the speed. In one poem, she says, "Guess any time that dying takes is slow." Here is Kathy Fagan's art: the faster we go, the sooner our hearts will open.

—Donald Sheehan

# The Weather They Were Written In

To start somewhere:
the window, ice, what fire
formed reformed
in frost, and frost itself
an other thing
more private somehow, and
complex, pinioned
like birds' underwings—
an arc and drift
of darkly plumaged peaks.

> In one pane, there's
> a kind of lake lain in
> among them, bevelled,
> small, but mostly clear,
> a peephole meant
> to see the cold through—weather
> that would surely
> liquefy your vision
> were you in it,
> weep things off to left

and right. But you
are not—out in it—
nor are you teary,
despite a robin, mirrored
in the glass,
who hurls his body at
his body, breathless
after each attempt.
He loves himself,
almost, to death, and who

> can blame him? His eyes

*are* lovely, his barrel
chest...! Look:
the logic of the male
cardinal
in snow is red that makes
the white bearable;
a chickadee's dressed
in birch tree's clothing;
and sparrow—little splinter,
little ash,
little antic where-
am-I—is little
but fat; she is too fat
in fact to fly,
and the sky is, anyhow,
too sharp
to fly through. Settle down
and think now. Didn't
Stevens write, of summer,
how what's solid
seems to vaporize,
denying form
or definition? And since
this is the opposite
of August, couldn't
smoke in winter prove
the converse may be
true? At least, a crow
has found a pillar
of it—stalled above
a chimney flue—
sure enough to huddle
near: a something
other, separate from,

by which to judge
and warm himself—a staggered
column, woodstove
smoke, that would be nothing
without its circumstance,
  the small flesh
  that needs it.

# To a Reader

What if I did not begin as I
used to? Here is the house
and its family, I said once;
here the bride, the grave,
and the window (*oh won't you*...).
What if loss and desire
were not a split curtain
ever parted and joined,
and the book never opened
to a leaf you had pressed there,
and I refused all
irony, which is,
of course, accommodation?

Yesterday three deer burst
out of the field I walked in—
a fine rain, snowcover,
mist that rose from the melting—
and though I know I was
meant to forget I
remembered not you most wholly
when the smallest one of them,
spotting me, stopped, bolted,
stopped again, spun round;
and since then assuredly
a choice had been made,
resumed its place in the vanishing.

# Driving It

By then it was late
Spring, and the medians and berms had that

Morning-after look about them: weedy, unshaven, vaguely
Obscene. Anyone could see

What a good drunk it had been.
It was all that green,

For one thing, set off by how the sprung
Confetti of dogwood clung

To the woods' edge, and how the birches stuck and glinted,
A quiver of bolts Neptune might have shot

Off, showing off. The sky too was turning opal
Forerunner of summer's usual

Milk—and like the stone its heart seemed shattered,
As if it were

At fault for snow
Cottonwoods in fact had made, letting their seedpods go.

I'd been driving. The bridge was out ahead.
No—the bridge ahead

Was under construction,
Traffic slow. We'd gotten

Used to it, inured:
The word

Itself a streak
On glass. So while the roadkill of the week

Before disturbed us, while it remained,
Uncannily, what it once had been—

Despite the neon
Orange X spraypainted on

Its back—we kept driving, stop-and-going,
And heard the river echoing

The drill when the drill quit.
Years ago, in Texas, my friend took us to visit

Austin's landmark,
Treaty Oak.

The tree had been poisoned—enormous,
Imploding, it looked, she said, like a house

Plant dying—and when I asked, rhetorically, *Who would
Do a thing like that*, shaking my head,

*Someone like God,*
Was what my friend said.

You see I drove that road every day. I didn't want to stop
Driving it. Someone blows up

A building, someone guts his muzzled pet,
Someone beats a child to death

And it's just more news
(And not) that loses

(And not) its horror by degrees. She's dead now, she
Was dying then. We didn't want to be

Used to it, but the bridge was
Out ahead, the sky was strange with snow. And there was

Something else as well, something almost delicate
In the arrangement of the corpse around the worksite.

Someone must have used his hands: the displays
Were too calculated to be achieved otherwise,

And anyone could see what a good
Job had been done. I drove that road

Every day. I didn't mind
The wait. I liked the treeline,

The undeveloped fields, the way, that time of year,
A cardinal said *Here I*
    *Here I*
    *Here I am am am am am am,*
Claiming he was everywhere,

That every place was his,
And every thing. Or that it would be. Even this.

# Blue

The sky is breathing birds this evening,
breathing them in and out of the light.
    From light to darkness, the breath of them rises,
the breath of them falls, the breasts of them glowing
    where the sun is.

─────────────

A sunset lasts where land is flattest.
    Where can it hide?

─────────────

But the needle in the flame
    and the skin it's burned for—
beneath them is a hidden fire:
    pilot light, blue and bluer,
like sky before the sun gets in,
    like blood in our veins before the needle.

─────────────

*Make straight in the desert a highway for our God...*
    and watch from it the sun on either side:
needle in the gas flame, sacred heart of the pilot light.

─────────────

    On this side, dusk, a pink
horizon, the amethyst it gets
    to be; and leafless trees—
plain as sparrow feathers here—
    are startled into light, like converts
or the damned.

─────────────

    I wanted to be Paolo *and* Francesca.
Not one or the other but the passion between them:
    sparrow, sycamore, jumbo jetliner—
what rises and sustains its rising, a lit thing

in remotest blue, shining in a blue
that never listens.

———————

    Flying in God's face, is what they said.
But if not there, O pilot light,
    where then will

———————

you fly? With the weightless dead
    at the end of the world?

———————

I've read that on All Hallow's Eve
    the line between life and death
is thinnest. Like this horizon here:
    *Make straight in the desert a needle and follow . . .*

———————

It's not the end of the world I'm thinking of
    but the other side:
the sky vein-blue and deaf still,
    not a bird in it, not a breath.
It will be morning there but not yet.
    I will be rising there but not yet.
For now, the sunset lasts and lasts,
    and there are, besides me, people watching.

# MOVING & ST RAGE

*—billboard on Ohio State Route 36*

Of course, something is missing,
which accounts for his sainthood, his legendary fury;
and while it would be false to say that Moving never dwelt
upon the source of that absence,
wondering what hand of god or man,
what rupture or obscuring force
might snatch a vowel from its rightful place,
                              shaping him thus, charting forever
the course of their merged destinies,
equally false would be to claim
she'd loved him any other way,
or that she was not drawn to Rage
as to the flame, and he to the sentiment
her name made: his lips mouthed roundly on her
                              first syllable, his jaw clenched
shut as he uttered the last; nor was the paradox lost
on them, susceptible as they were to words,
and symbols, like the ampersand,
cousin to the treble clef,
whose plainer features also set
the pitch and tumble of mortal endeavor,
                              and joined these two like ones before
who'd met on the grassy medians of myth
to pledge those troths the gods grow jealous of:
there are limits placed on endless love.

And that is why Rage came to travel, and walks
the foreign seacoast of an ancient city now,
anonymous among the crowds, and through a speech so vastly
                              strange, it does not interrupt his reverie;

nothing can: not the whirl of birds and white
umbrellas in the sun of the *platia*, not the darkly pretty twining couples
espaliering ocher walls—all's to Rage
a froth and sway he cannot comprehend;
and useless as it is to question
which of them felt banished first, or when
                              their hardening of hearts began
like the fortification of separate kingdoms,
question they must, Rage & Moving, cursed to live
beyond their primes, and one half-day and -world apart,
to ride a wheel of common failures
that is hope turning up
and regret coming down, and that makes a sound like
                    *See Me   See Me,*
spewing grit and salt and stars, grinding
on its dark axis—and while she knows that Earth
itself has blocked the moon she loves from sight,
Moving can't recall tonight the reason
bodies spin this way, or who first named the blank
moon New, believed an unlit promise with a faith
                    the there-not-there was whole,

and not a lost and gone forever, hugely missed and missing O.

# CHRISTOPHER GILBERT

## 1986

Christopher Gilbert touches a quality in his work that Charles Olsen, the great projectivist poet, once called "the use a person makes of himself, hence, makes of others." Olsen said, "If a man sprawls he shall have little to sing but of himself, but if he stays inside himself, if he is contained within his nature, he will be able to listen and his hearing through himself will give him, through himself, the secret objects share." In his poems, Christopher Gilbert exhibits this remarkable self-possession, this power to listen, and to listen all the way.

—Donald Sheehan

# Tourist (Walking at The Robert Frost Place)

Because it is the route that is the work
I could take the world itself to mean
myself. Into these hills that happen abruptly
like the present, I could take place and be one
with the subject of my feeling arising
before me. The way the Queen's Lace sways
could be an indication of my breath
coming and going. As if an outline for time
itself, here I am stepping forth as an instance
walking the mountain road to the hilltop where
around the bend I'll hear someone working
on a house the frame of whose part—the material
and the aesthetic and their perishing—linked
together will stand for history. It is
July 4th, the goldenrod popping
at the road's edge, the daisies all over
exploding with white rays, the coltsfoot buttery,
and nodding thistle rose-purple everywhere
itself, the little water in the wind
all at once reminding me of myself. I am
into small steps here—I total the bits of me
I have lived in office places, dispirited,
without song, and no hill of time ahead
into whose doors a man could walk and be
transformed, believing, local, and facing the sky.
Now I am nearing the end of my youth, not
nearly the person I thought I would be
not half my life ago when I was ripe with
renegade outbreaks of energy for *doing*
*something*, searching for a home for the empathy
that would be me, Armstrong walking the nearer

moon and me hot headed, twenty, with
a future seeming never too soon, seed
whose crazed circumstance among things yielded
its mysterious blossoming. Now the people
passing me in their cars, faces red and
pink swollen like the climbing bittersweet
berries, bouncing up and down like dice
in trustless boxes, might just as well be me
caught in a body no where completely
at home. The little water in the wind
reminds me of my sorrow, a quick gust
I can't explain. What is happening is me
even as I see the Bee Balm's bright star
call the hummingbird into its circle,
even as every doubt I am is my flowing
home that you have called me into, world.

# A Sorrow Since Sitting Bull

Dust on the horizon,
whirlwind, whirlwind blown
in the globe of your eye
where you sit in the back
of the pick-up, facing back,
with your reservation a skin
surrounding you, with a warm Bud
in your hand, with the where-
the-dirt-road-leads beneath you
spun up as the wheels spin around
till the present narrows to nothing
at the horizon.

The yankee shops everywhere—
like a ring around your life—
sell beadwork, jade, bottled spirit.
Dust on the horizon, you wait
for a wind to bring the buffalo back.
Nothing comes, not even a job.
A gust circles here in lament.
It doubles, reeding in the gut
of the grasses that have become this road:
*All Your Relations Are Ghosts*
*in the Truck with You.* Faithful you,
you ride on into the future,
facing back, facing back.

—*for Leona One Feather*

# The Plum

The way the music is seeing inside. Where the seeing is enclosed the way the world is enclosed within the dark lid of the African god's eye. Where the note is a fruit whose flesh is darker than the mass filling the eye. It's the vision itself. And I'm closed onto myself.

Seen from the top my sensuousness is the shape of two rubied lips forming a kiss or else the blush around the purplish syllable which all but two similar lips mistake as sex's squish. The sound of the tenderest trembling spreads throughout me. I grow up flush with the deep anticipation holed up in the opening of a bell. I ripen and am the living resolve that sweetens in the vase of death, and am the seed that leads deeper down into the play of melody.

◆

Thelonious Monk is reaching for a note. A goal he already has in his inner grasp. He cups this plum in the palm of his hand, and makes that hesitation during which the music is a motion which sleeps. And for an instant his eye and his plum are alone in the world, and not regarding each other except through that live space that connects two minds or planets. He's living off a vision. The death is illuminated where he sees, and it wakes. He's rewarding himself with a plum. When he plays he's feeding himself with himself.

# To Get to My Extreme

Threading through
Our black bodies, in-
Complete sacred seeking,
Tentative stepping

Ain't dancin' dancin'
Black language! The
Landscape lighting up
Ahead of us,

Unfolding
Amidst oblique partners
And their short
Memories,

With each step
A moment breaks
And something else
Becomes old science.

For example,
I walk the streets'
Bye bye, to get to
The line's end.

By Monet, not
Geometry, green
And yellow weightless
Stars, behind each other

Depthless under a bridge.
By Bartok, not
Plato's whiteness, reconciling
Here with whatever

My dark hunger says.
Put yo' arms
Around me, baby.
Put yo' arms around me.

The fingers frolic
Filling with myself,
My gestures merge with meaning
The sky around me,

Speaking black,
Radio falling from my mouth
To get to
My extreme.

For example,
I get vanished
Rapped up
In my lyric.

Subject to the nighttime's
Pretty utterance,
I open my mouth, not taking
Nobody's words for it.

# Leaving the Loop, 1992

To get into what is wasted with this year
is to be a Black man in your life's time,
which is to play *So What* everyday
from your birth step to your death step
a million different ways, which is to know
in the skin the trouble with now
where nobody stands up to time
anymore—at least not long enough
to make it a joke, at least not
hard enough to fuck with subsequently
and like and thus to see and so forth
coming but mean to hell with stepping aside.

You were middle of this century so
what at turning your back to Frazier's black
bourgeoisie, the white country-clubbers, the half un-
hinged hipster night club scene, the dizzy
New York manual of style. You were showing
your back to us—so macho: aloof, oblique, cool.
Middle of this century you were so
what the whole system is Wittgensteinian
put-on as the holy wear in tribute
toward the black river of song. You spat
into the river as you flowed along, a source
never going no where but always coming to

form—this *here*, this *now*, this *depth*, more *You*.
Outside the loop, hearing, "Nothing but
the framework, boys." It all was equipment
to you: your women, your horn, your song, even you.
Sullen, silent, deep blue. Always showing

your back to us—such leaving: alone, legato, lamenting.
Wasn't it Orpheus had himself remember
by taking shape in the notes you blew?
But so what? Don't the members got you down?
We shrug our shoulders as we each die.
You doggone dead ass "nother brother." *So What.*
You goddamned bad ass trumpet master. *So What.*
You flow breaking into complex modulated cry.

# A Metaphor for Something That Plays Us

*(Remembering Eric Dolphy)*

Legend, you made up map of acts
getting it right in the record, awed attention
mending itself into memory to become this moment
issuing its tissue of circumstances inside us.
It all starts with longing and then working it out,
letting the space for the story set itself up
so that the presence can come into its own to me.
So I'm filled with eighties longing and walking
as I carve my nerve out of this dumb decade, making my way
through a park of Dutch diseased elms, the untimely death
a generation ago of Eric Dolphy on my mind.
When a young bird's plaintive cry—an evanescent
burst from the chest—asks that I hear its singing,
my empty breath falls short while what's going on
in the trees grows large with the regard that the rustling of
the leaves is an expression for. Everything becoming
backdrop, even the traffic at the corner
up ahead in the future where the park ends
mimics a chorus humming at full stop.

Listen. Hear how the meaning of each moment is
the dialect gained when the future assumes the flesh.
I traipse through trash thickets where
the acting president's civil wrongs have trickled down.
Humming what bits I can of "Out to Lunch,"
by the time I get to a bench at the park's edge
where the traffic's strict metronomic
thickens to bicker against the music
in my head, I feel sick—my route afflicted
with the day's euphoric waste that I must fight

else it fills me to the quick, But listen,
even the righteous tire of trying to get it right.
The way we'd like to be like that pure interest, like
that wild witness who uses the caustic specs
of this false nature but is not a victim of the mess.
Bold, absorbed bystander! We made Dolphy into that,
and where did it leave him. So out of this world,
a bothered god in his music, against the lavish nothing
mass produced by the uniformity of the Coldwar culture,
he sank into history, estranged, a soloist
worshipping in an orchestra of indifference.
That was not his fact, a striving
thing standing beside himself in light of the times—
bud, breath, beautiful momentary being—
a demo of the striving. Undoing
the definition of the diatonic scale, or
displaying his life as a voice, his only future
was to invent a language where he became
his own name pouring from the mouth of his horn.
So much the music in this human world
he never had an audience, never
found an other who could talk back.

Man we mess it all up! We step forward
into our urban selves all faithless and fashionable
as though living were a paint job, a lie—
that put-on face which has its moment that
then, like an uncoded character left
in the oblivious weather, simply fades away.
Behind Dolphy's music was Dolphy's music
forever; so there was something abiding being
said. Here's a songbird's call, a flute's bent plea,
melts into wail, gathers to pour from
the mouth of the teenager who, I will say,

has come to this park to be
alone because it all feels wrong at home.
I walk closer to the traffic's noise
and see my face in the driver's seat
in a Chevy streaking away from me, and
in this instant it seems that none of this—
the bird's cry, the flute's plea, the runaway,
Dolphy, this passing moment, or I—
amounts to more than a picture
splintering here into dust and time,
where each blue feeling is like a word's
sound when it is read to no one.
Yet when I remember Dolphy I am
aware of myself humming a set of notes
whose sequence tells a story that I become
avowal for. Just as, out of attention,
when you say these words I am brought
to mind, the practice of the tenderness
you have become a witness for.

# PATTIANN ROGERS

## 1987

In her work, Pattiann Rogers combines the two great ends of all poetry, perhaps of all art: passion and precision. As to precision, she uses very easily, very fluently, and very exactly the languages of what we know as the descriptive sciences, the languages of botany, geology, biology, and physics. And in this sense her poems approach the world as a naturalist would approach it. But the themes of her poems are often beyond the describable world, and the tiny creatures in her poems—the mice, the insects, the tiny geological process that she charts so exactly—become emblems of the great world. What's most moving and beautiful in her work is that we learn to see this great world only when we become still enough to see these small things exactly. And the result is art of great fineness and of great power.

—Donald Sheehan

# Elinor Frost's Marble-Topped Kneading Table

Imagine that motion, the turning and pressing,
the constant folding and overlapping, the dough
swallowing and swallowing and swallowing itself
again, just as the sea, bellying up the hard shore,
draws back under its own next forward-moving
roll, slides out from under itself
along the beach and back again; that first
motion, I mean, like the initial act
of any ovum (falcon, leopard, crab) turning
into itself, taking all of its outside surfaces
inward; the same circular mixing and churning
and straightening out again seen at the core
of thunderheads born above deserts; that involution
ritualized inside amaryllis bulbs
and castor beans in May.

Regard those hands now, if you never
noticed before, flour-caked fists and palms knuckling
the lump, gathering, dividing, tucking
and rolling, smoothing, reversing. I know,
from the stirring and sinking habits
of your own passions, that you recognize
this motion.

And far in the distance, (you may even
have guessed) far past Orion and Magellan's vapors,
past the dark nebulae and the sifted rings
of interstellar dust, way beyond mass and propulsion,
before the first wheels and orbits of sleep
and awareness, there, inside that moment
which comes to be, when we remember,

at the only center where it has always been,
an aproned figure stands kneading, ripe
with yeast, her children at her skirts.
Now and then she pauses, bends quickly,
clangs open the door, tosses another stick
on the fire.

# The Significance of Location

The cat has the chance to make the sunlight
Beautiful, to stop it and turn it immediately
Into black fur and motion, to take it
As shifting branch and brown feather
Into the back of the brain forever.

The cardinal has flown the sun in red
Through the oak forest to the lawn.
The finch has caught it in yellow
And taken it among the thorns. By the spider
It has been bound tightly and tied
In an eight-stringed knot.

The sun has been intercepted in its one
Basic state and changed to a million varieties
Of green stick and tassle. It has been broken
Into pieces by glass rings, by mist
Over the river. Its heat
Has been given the board fence for body,
The desert rock for fact. On winter hills
It has been laid down in white like a martyr.

This afternoon we could spread gold scarves
Clear across the field and say in truth,
"Sun you are silk."

Imagine the sun totally isolated,
Its brightness shot in continuous streaks straight out
Into the black, never arrested,
Never once being made light.

Someone should take note
Of how the earth has saved the sun from oblivion.

# Rolling Naked in the Morning Dew

Out among the wet grasses and wild barley-covered
Meadows, backside, frontside, through the white clover
And feather peabush, over spongy tussocks
And shaggy-mane mushrooms, the abandoned nests
Of larks and bobolinks, face to face
With vole trails, snail niches, jelly
Slug eggs; or in a stone-walled garden, level
With the stemmed bulbs of orange and scarlet tulips,
Cricket carcasses, the bent blossoms of sweet william,
Shoulder over shoulder, leg over leg, clear
To the ferny edge of the goldfish pond—some people
Believe in the rejuvenating powers of this act—naked
As a toad in the forest, belly and hips, thighs
And ankles drenched in the dew-filled gulches
Of oak leaves, in the soft fall beneath yellow birches,
All of the skin exposed directly to the killy cry
Of the king bird, the buzzing of grasshopper sparrows,
Those calls merging with the dawn-red mists
Of crimson steeplebush, entering the bare body then
Not merely through the ears but through the skin
Of every naked person willing every event and potentiality
Of a damp transforming dawn to enter.

Lillie Langtry practiced it, when weather permitted,
Lying down naked every morning in the dew,
With all of her beauty believing the single petal
Of her white skin could absorb and assume
That radiating purity of liquid and light.
And I admit to believing myself, without question,
In the magical powers of dew on the cheeks
And breasts of Lillie Langtry believing devotedly

In the magical powers of early morning dew on the skin
Of her body lolling in purple beds of bird's-foot violets,
Pink prairie mimosa. And I believe, without doubt,
In the mystery of the healing energy coming
From that wholehearted belief in the beneficent results
Of the good delights of the naked body rolling
And rolling through all the silked and sun-filled,
Dusky-winged, sheathed and sparkled, looped
And dizzied effluences of each dawn
Of the rolling earth.

Just consider how the mere idea of it alone
Has already caused me to sing and sing
This whole morning long.

# The Hummingbird: A Seduction

If I were a female hummingbird perched still
And quiet on an upper myrtle branch
In the spring afternoon and if you were a male
Alone in the white heavens before me, having parted
Yourself, for me, from cedar top and honeysuckle stem
And earth down, your body hovering in midair
Far away from jewelweed, thistle and bee balm;

And if I watched how you fell, plummeting before me,
And how you rose again and fell, with such mastery
That I believed for a moment you were the sky
And the red-marked bird diving inside your circumference
Was just the physical revelation of the light's
Most perfect desire;

And if I saw your sweeping and sucking
Performance of swirling egg and semen in the air,
The weaving, twisting vision of red petal
And nectar and soaring rump, the rush of your wing
In its grand confusion of arcing and splitting
Created completely out of nothing just for me,

Then when you came down to me, I would call you
My own spinning bloom of ruby sage, my funneling
Storm of sunlit sperm and pollen, my only breathless
Piece of scarlet sky, and I would bless the base
Of each of your feathers and touch the tine
Of string muscles binding your wings and taste
The odor of your glistening oils and hunt
The honey in your crimson flare
And I would take you and take you and take you
Deep into any kind of nest you ever wanted.

# Predestination

I don't know how the wood thrush knows
how to match the pitch and fall of its cry
exactly to the pitch and fall the mountain ridge
makes against the evening sky.

And I don't know how the purple bee balm
knows how to pattern the spray and spread
of its spear-pointed blossoms exactly to the thrust
and parry, the petal-thin whirr and circling
thrimble of the hunting hummingbird.

Each round lobe of three-leafed clover
fits itself perfectly into each green note
of the treefrog's treble, and each treefrog
swells its tremolo in cylindrical bunches
of three-toned rings.

The warblers, all together, place their calls
as leaf upon leaf of forest overlay
and shadow. And see how the black branches
of the spruce against the gray sky
have shaped themselves in their ascent
to the same spikes and needles
the black dog yelps
from his chain beside the shed.

What is it that I imitate? to what structure
do I meld? my stance, my cry and mumble
fitting exactly into the chinks
and snugness of some *other*? What is it
that makes its own body, that finds the steps

of its own motion against the outline
of my voice?

There must be something. There must.
Since my conviction may be
its very stature and its very spine,
how can I be convinced otherwise?

# Abundance and Satisfaction

1.

One butterfly is not enough. We need
many thousands of them, if only
for the effusion of the wayward-
swaying words they occasion—blue
and copper hairstreaks, sulphur
and cabbage whites, brimstones,
peacock fritillaries, tortoiseshell
emperors, skippers, meadow browns.
We need a multitude of butterflies
right on the tongue simply to be able
to speak with a varied six-pinned
poise and particularity.

But thousands of butterflies
are surfeit. We need just one
flitter to apprehend correctly
the will of aspen leaves, the lassitude
of lupine petals, the sleep
of a sleeping eyelid. To examine
adequately one set of finely leaded,
stained wings of violet translucence,
one single sucking proboscis (sap-
and-sugar-licking thread), to study
thoroughly just one powder scale, one
gold speck from one dusted butterfly
forewing would require at least
a millennium of attention to all melody,
phrase, gravity and horizon.

2.

And just the same, one moon is more
than sufficient, ample complexity
and bewilderment—single waning crescent,
waxing crescent, lone gibbous, one perfect,
solitary sickle and pearl, one map
of mountains and lava plains, Mare
Nectaris, Crater Tycho. And how could
anyone really hold more than one full
moon in one heart?

Yet one moon is not enough. We need
millions of moons, glassy porcelain
globes glowing as if from the inside out,
weaving among each other in the sky
like lanterns bobbing on a black river
sea-bound. Then we could study
moons and the traversings of moons
and the multiple meanings of the phases
of moons, and the eclipsing of moons
by one another. We need a new language
of moons containing all the syllables
of interacting rocks of light
so that we might fully understand,
at last, the phrase "one heart
in many moons."

3.

And of gods, we need just one, one
for the grief of twenty snow geese
frozen by their feet in ice and dead

above winter water. Yet we need twenty-
times-twenty gods for all the recurring
memories of twenty snow geese frozen
by their feet in sharp lake-water ice.

But a single god suffices
for the union of joys in one school
of invisible green-brown minnows
flocking over green-brown stones
in a clear spring, but three gods
are required to wind and unwind
the braided urging of spring—root,
blossom and spore. And we need
the one brother of gods for a fragged
plain, blizzard-split, battered
by tumbleweeds and wire fences,
and the one sister to mind
the million sparks and explosions
of gods on fire in a pine forest.

I want one god to be both scatter
and pillar, one to explain simultaneously
mercy and derision, yet a legion of gods
for the spools of confusion and design,
but one god alone to hold me by the waist,
to rumble and quake in my ear, to dance me
round and round, one couple with forty
gods in the heavenly background
with forty violins with one
immortal baton keeping time

# JOHN ENGELS

## 1988

John Engels has five children who are now in their thirties and forties. It's this fact that connects to a very important quality in his work. There's a very beautiful German word, *Bodenständigkeit*, which means "homesteadiness," a quality of staying with something, a sound, an image; of staying with it past the point where it's glamorous and exciting to be with it, to a point where it's true, it's deeply true. Of being at home in it. There's a line from Rilke's marvelous novel *Malte Laurids Brigge*: "My God, so you really *are*." Such is the effect of John Engels's work: it really is.

—Donald Sheehan

# Ghosts

The looming thing
that moved against me all night long
still lives in the hallway when,
shoes in hand, I limp to the door

and peer out. Then through the wings
of sluggish shadow that it is
spread bright fragrances—
sweet breads, bacon, eggs frying

in the sunny kitchen and I
cannot go down, I'm frightened to go down,
seeing I have dreamed all night

of birds, of the dogs
of my growing up, my mother
at twenty, my father

among soldiers, thinking
I would hear their voices
for the last time; and hearing them.

# Landslide

By first light the pines struck down into the meadow.
Only an hour before the clouds had been heavy, shadows
       buried the rafters, and light scurried
   window to window. But then
       the snow began to flicker, clouds to deform,
  and from the incandescent line of the peak
proceeded a ragged scrolling of light, finally
  the sun itself clearing the highest ridge,
       bearing with it a wind so violent
  that nothing in the stunned world knew more
       than that something must have changed. At 5 A.M.,
the house cold, cold light billowing and the hibiscus
  abloom in the north window, dark clouds low,
       gold-bellied over the snowy yard, the sky
  paling and bold against it two engorged blossoms
  back-lit by snowshine, star-hearted purple-to-vermilion
       where the petals overlapped, I looked up at the mountain
and from just beneath the shoulder of one shimmering ridge

    occurred an abrupt enlargement of shadow
       from out of which the mountain stormed,
  bearing before it colossal froth of mud, boulders, trees,
  bright explosions of brooks and ponds, snow clouds, all
soundless, therefore suggesting nothing of danger
  so that I felt no need to run
       before the landslide until at last
  it cascaded over the head wall into the valley
and crested in a roar of dust and snow
at the road's crown and overran
the house where I had been standing at the porch window
  brave with amazement. Too late

I discovered myself to have failed
 to escape, to have been borne down
  by house and mountain, my cheek
 crushed into a sour linoleum, my breath
  irretrievable, on my eyelids ant,
earwig, spider, the house above me still
 and orderly in ruin that theretofore most ordinary
  of all mornings when merely to have looked
up at the mountain from the swollen buds
and blooms of the hibiscus, of all things red
 most red, had been enough
  to commence the overbalancing
 into that swirl, billow, upheaving dome
of ice and shadow where I was about to die,
 or was already dead, or must describe
which it was to be.

—*for Don Sheehan*

# Wakeful at Midnight

Do you pray to be safe,
rendered without interest
to whatever in your house, hiddenly at play
and otherwise incurious, might pause

in its doings, consider, sharpen its notice, horribly
attend you? How readily on stairwells
do you turn your back? On cellar doors,
on the unlockable closets? Do you live

in terror of the coldness of attics?
Midnights, certain the unearthly light
moves room by room closer to where
you have failed to sleep,
how can you not believe

that the darkness flowering about you
will soon pose limits to itself,
that you will be sought out?

*—at The Frost Place, August 1989*

# The Dead

My grandmother was 85
when she fell and broke her hip
and lay another two years
the rest of her life
in a hospital bed

they came to her
all of them: Leon, her husband, dead
ten years by then, Etta
and Ella, the sisters, Lloyd,
fast-talking huckster for whatever
needed selling (TV antennas, aluminum

siding, brooms and brushes)
but who failed in his last pitch
and ended up in a thicket of blackberry bushes
along the back road to Bawbeese Lake. And Eleanore,
my mother, dead young and early

out of some bitter
sequestered justice—and there they were,
no question, she followed them
with her eyes, turned her head on the pillow
to this corner and that, to the chair
beside her bed, to the doorway, greeted

them when they arrived, and said goodbye,
held their hands, chatted happily
about this pattern of chintz, a recipe
for molasses cookies, the leak

no one could fix in the old rowboat,
made plans and appointments . . . she was happy

those last days when they came to her
or rather must have seemed
never to have left. Only we were not

happy, and our selfsame dead
hadn't the time of day to spare for us
who kept them far away, beyond
any least danger of retrieval, we

who wept at loss and memory,
and for her old dear body
helpless in the bed, but most of all from fear
they might after all take notice, turn
and speak to us, require regeneration
of that difficult love we gave them once
that from the very beginning
imperceptibly altered itself
into the final language, this passionate strange discourse
of fear and mourning.

# Poem for Your Birthday

Time is so ceremonious, stately
in greeting, full of congratulation,
exquisite in manner, insistent
on protocol (place settings

just so, right down
to fish knives, asparagus forks,
the crispest of linens, every candle
perfectly upright and burning

at precisely the same rate) And above all Time
is orderly, never mind

the coil and swirl of counter currents
in the sullen pantries, the mutterings
of servants…these
he ignores. But now here you are at last

once more as every year
arrived at this party, at this door,
outside in the soft night watching
the windows brighten and darken

with the shadows of the other guests
who've come on time, watching his windows
flicker with candles; and you hear
their polite murmurings, their small

swellings of applause, and then
silence as the cake enters

grand in the coronal aura of its light.
Though you are very late,

you halt at the door. You can choose, if you like,
to not go in at all. But after all
you suffer obligation, you've been invited,
found yourself unable

to refuse. Still
you hesitate, though you know
he knows you're there, your hand
hesitant on the bell. Yet, forever tactful,

he waits for you to ring, he understands
the embarrassment you'd feel
should the door open on you
in your reluctance. You must

make up your mind. Fear fidgets
in your breast, but then goes stolid
and assured. Nevertheless you must
make up your mind. Everyone's

been waiting, the food is gone,
and the cake is ready
to be cut. You must decide, must do your best
to require of your heart

that just for the moment
it overwhelm doubt, and seem joyous. Try
to look forward to Time's greeting: knock
and be admitted. After all, what is the worst

that can happen? He will do no more
than open the door to you, and stand there,
slim, elegant, eyes hooded and welcoming,
forever courteous. He will not

reproach you. Rest assured
your comfort and enjoyment
will be everything to him.

# My Mother's Heritage

I have this from you: a dislike
of severity: you gave me over
helpless to motley and gorgeous

scatterings of stuffs, our house
folds and drapings of old brocades
cut velvet throws, light

unfocused and flowering back
in warm petals of brightness from lustre cups
and pitchers, bowls and plates,

potpourri everywhere (pine cones,
rose petals, lavender and cinnamon)
French needlepoint and porcelains, mercury

and Bristol glass in all
the cupboards. And Chinese lacquer, brasses
everywhere: Belgian

bedwarmers, candlesticks
platters and sconces . . . I dazzled
and staggered through your rooms

then out, and far away, gathered
and took them with me. And here
I am today, primed for the joyous confusion

I hope for: dusty light, and every corner
forever beautifully unsquared.

# Rising Stream

At first only a scattered drift of twigs and leaves
in the main thread of the current, then
little rafts of yellow foam, and something angular

and unnatural in the downstream sweep
and belly of the line. But I was intent
on the rise against the far bank

just under the overdroop
of a black willow, a big rainbow
rising to ants, and I narrowed

and worried myself to the angles,
light, shadows, fly and drag, until
it caught me that the lower branches of the tree

had begun to trail in the current
and that I was bracing myself
against the river, and that suddenly

the stream was wider, higher
on the banks, and I started
to get out of there, and made it,

and stood for awhile on the bank
watching that wild growth, watching the river
thicken with its old muds

and swirl and bubble and foam with vapor,
deeper than I was tall where I had stood—
and here I stand, telling you

about it—how that gradual power of river
built and bore down on me
and might have drowned me.

I tell you, over the years
out of obscure purpose I've made it to seem
it came up on me with purpose,

had me marked down
for the big eddy of driftwood
just out of sight around the bend.

The cold smell of that water comes to me
over and over in a dream, sometimes,
especially, these days, when I'm otherwise

wide awake, the smell of that day
chill and sour, and oddly
flavored, like fresh earth.

# JULIE AGOOS

## 1989

I n her poems, Julie Agoos steadily holds the densities of experience and thought in a rich intelligence—working between clear plainness and the inchoate, the darkly resistant. In this, she has become one of our few Senecan poets. Seneca, that immensely interesting Roman poet, is one we need to read anew. For Seneca says, in a late letter, that "greatness of soul" is achieved when we do a thing with "order, measure, fitness [Latin: *decor*], and a will that is non-toxic and compassionate." Julie Agoos's poems touch this Senecan greatness of soul—and therefore they greatly touch us.

—Donald Sheehan

# Delphinium

"...this blue consolidating, as it were, from air...
frail stalks claiming their final territory
at the crossroads that my looking guards
against their rich expansion: everywhere
a blue that cannot be ignored is swaying
beyond its borders where the next few will,
a few days off, gather, skeletal;
begin the forceful pressure to exist.

"Then, always surprised by what I had not noticed,
my imagination will grow more than wishful: hard.
Surprise turn into expectation soon enough.

"So, for two or three days, as they come on
in a blue mist—calling my attention first
far beyond them, to the ridge—I'd make them
disappear, or let them disappear
and call the mountains back. But even then
I could not keep peripheral the fact
that what I overlooked was growing loud
(rich, perfect height—serene, almost objective
in a vase) inside the house again—

"...so that I fear I can't escape, hard as I try;
that I cannot be more faithful than they are."

# Lowell House, Taunton Hill

Like one of the old ones who have outlived their fathers,
who do not know each other, but know each others' names
—origins that frame the little town
in generous distance nothing can control—
the house is settled under maple trees
in late October, early afternoon,
aloof in the knowledge of what will not change:
The mountain, the cemetery, the dark road
full of shadow, and the rough lawn,
covered up in leaves, as darkly furrowed,
only the orchard side made invisible
yet the mind seeing clear around the house
—a trick of symmetry he tried a hundred times
before turning to the final tempera.
To borrow the key and enter now
would unleash the violence of that poorer age;
the road keeps close to ignorance,
a few low clouds lifting off the mountain,
the fence around the cemetery gleaming
where the faint sun finds it in the northeast.
The house, green-shuttered, violet-white, four-sided,
has never been kept by anyone, and still
it is the house the town is proudest of.
I look at it and think that loneliness
has no part in such peace, in which alone it seems
unlike any person one might ever know.

# Portrait from Senlis

The first time that I saw her I was shy:
Madame Duranti in her rocking chair,
dusting her slippered feet along one square
of tiled floor. Then, looking up, she stared,
beckoning with a cigarette, gold-tipped,
and indicated where I ought to sit
without a word of welcome. Arch face lit,
she discoursed roughly, in a mannish way,
on furniture from Asia, rocks, how day-
light hit peculiarly the window bay.
"An invalid," she said, "should never wed.
Why bother with a husband, when instead
a doctor keeps you company in bed?"
And laughed and said, "It's crude, but so am I."

Madame received on Sundays, knowing I
was easy in her high-walled room and played
piano she might listen to. I stayed
for dinner on the nights she was afraid
to be alone, not out of charity
but gratified that she felt safe with me,
so fascinated by her dignity
I would have stayed a month, though she delighted
in declaring she abhorred the self-invited.
And when she said, "You *know* I'm second-sighted?"
I said, "*Tell me*—" but she laughed and said, "I lie."

She was never overbearing; still, with pride
she graciously received and from her bed
directed whiskey to be poured, and read
descriptions from a travel guide. She said,

"One must see everything, and when one's through,
one must *try* everything, then do
as much again. You see? I'm telling you
that God created man to travel and
you must decide—" Then, stretching out her hand—
"And be content to die if not a man
and not a minute has escaped your eye."

# An Afternoon's Activity

*—for Peter and David Michaelis*

All night the train, no sleep, the deaf conductor
shouting to us at Tarantella.
We left there, and come here, sleepwalkers.

> *In dreams, each plane*
> *rising and roaring*
> *or in a descent*
> *too steep to dare the land*
> *heads for the ocean.*
> *I am frozen passenger,*
> *feeling a steady heat*
> *beneath my ribs.*

Above the door there are three red stars.
"Caveat Emptor," Diana says, alert,
"o sono queste le porte del Paradiso?
If not, we could do ourselves a lot of harm."

> *Awake, I cannot*
> *reconstruct*
> *what sea it was,*
> *what land the flight*
> *had come from; why*
> *I feel hope and fear.*

Still we go in through this *porta principale*,
passing our bags to the solemn *portiere*
("chi porta un fiore all'occhiello, vedi?")
and whose gait (*portamento*), with its
slow preamble, makes us laugh some more.

*Never mind, never mind.*
*Dio, ho fame.*

Later we find it's just a guidebook rating
Meaning: the best (*il migliore*) to indicate
that we should stay and eat. And in the vaulted
cellar, where the fat cook keeps
a mythic rule (forbidding all talk except
on the subject of food), the young *camerieri*
strut table to table, *e ci domandano*
*cosa possono portare.* "Che inferno,"
Diana says, removing her red shawl.

> *Trees flare. Outside*
> *my son's window*
> *planes of the upright*
> *oak tree romance*
> *the passive pine.*
> *And from the maple*
> *three red leaves*
> *fall and scatter.*
> *Their shadows blush*
> *on his young cheek*
> *as he bends to write me,*
> *while on the table,*
> *everything I own*
> *makes claims on him:*
> *the flask of yellow*
> *oil bellied out*
> *beside the orchid-full;*
> *the pumpkin china plates;*
> *pitcher and winestems*
> *ribboned round*

*with purple overflows;*
*dunes of linen!*

Then in the afternoon, I leave her nested
in blankets in the small bed beside
the *portafinestra* and the *portacatino*.
"I think I've found my port of call," she says,
flipping through the pages of her thick
*vocabolario*; and I take this as a great
sign of health, and tell her so. "You can think
what you like, so long as it brings me luck," she answers,
"but maybe you should get it down in writing.
At least we can give the postman something to do." *Tua*
*madre si sente di essere in porto,*
the postcard I will write next says.

*O let the sudden*
*quilting of the leaves*
*be respite to him!*

But going out of the Porta Rosa, doors
that I do not remember opening beget
more doors—just as those wooden child-women
open and reveal more children: through the lens
of anterooms, barren of all but a stray *portaombrelli*,
from each slow arch, the hazy sinopia
of mother and child with flowers holds me in its gaze,
eyes collapsed as if the world were nothing to them
now that they no longer have the power to move.

*By my son's flushed*
*cheek, the colorless*
*window is discreet*

*as midafternoon.*
*Light enters*
*as fairies are said to,*
*unafraid to sink*
*between disorders;*
*in the green half-bottles*
*turning the tension lines*
*like wine to acid.*
*I wake up worried,*
*feeling selfish.*

Nothing moves at two in the piazza:
white statues bronze under the dry
spirals of *sole, fontana.* Even the postcard
flat on the green bench could be from you
or for you, could be a plaque to someone: permanent.
Without tea or passersby, what
I see the only incremental changes:
cars where no cars were; a cloud of bicyclists
backpedalling by the curb, who race for distance,
and whose loud and unexpected voices
journey much as the eye does, as free
at times within the empty space the body fills.
Carried here without intention, or any real meaning,
They are at once foreign and heartbreaking.

"Sì, può portarci molto danno, la vita,"
like this strange genealogy of hours
in which already she has formed a middleground,
a place where all the pretty roots of words are,
between that small room with its empty
portafiori (*flower stand*) and this unused daylight
I have walked into without her.

The sun in my lap as I try writing this postcard
is an exclamation mark (punto),
an emphasis of what the sun was.

> *O, figlio,*
> *I am not*
> *beautiful, here,*
> *portando gli occhiali*
> *hanging on*
> *my swelled bosom*
> Herald International
> *spilled across*
> *my knees, portacappelli,*
> *portacarte,*
> *portacipria,*
> *portafogli,*
> *portacenere,*
> *portafrutta,*
> *everything still*
> *strewn everywhere*
> *around me. O,*
> *che letto di rose!*
> *Ma spero che stia*
> *in ogni caso*
> *alle porte*
> *quando arrivano*
> *queste lettere,*
> *quando arriverò,*
> *e quando vado via.*

# Intensive

Purple, scarlet, white anemones—
brilliance like paint's. Against the vase,
the three dimensions spill
into a waterfall.

*Christ!* the word was all; stale lips
purple when he spat it out.
And I: "That's him!", the ghost-flesh
gone again, machined

in the fluid swirl of the green-curtained room.
I didn't mean to hurt him," said
the nurse who had pinched
the soft lobe, and

recovered pain's odd naturalness: "Kee-*Rist!*"
familiar miracle of breath—
the golden flash or two
of strange joy. We knew—

having seen, as well, this scarlet light, the white
dropping to dust; a purple pale
and delicate, whose beauty was
in being first

and last, the black vase sheer and difficult
that stinks of its own reason: we are temporal.
Every inward chance
breaks free of us.

# ROSANNA WARREN

## 1990

I n her work, Rosanna Warren combines the skill of lyrical finish with the daringness of emotional and even spiritual risk. She allows into her poems other voices, other presences, other personalities that are not her own. And yet the experience is deeply unifying. There is a mystery in this. Thomas A. Kempis, the mystical writer, said, "[W]e should not trust too much to ourselves because we have often neither grace nor understanding." In her poems, Rosanna Warren points with a fineness and an alertness the way to a lovely grace and a fine understanding.

—Donald Sheehan

# Mountain View

*(Franconia, New Hampshire)*

Evening pulls a counterpane of shadow over Lafayette
outlining vertebrae, steep shoulder blades, groin,
and clustered here at the porch, tiger lilies and lupin
squeeze petals softly inward, enclosing twilight.

Last bird twitters fringe the meadow. I am alone
drawing the hour slowly around my shoulders,
hugging hunger as dusk drifts down and bewilders
the notebook page, its school-careful lines, the pen

motionless now as I pause and watch a biplane
hoist a glider into the virtual sky.
From the house down the road rises a child's cry.
The plane and its charge pass out of my field of vision,

they will release one another soon into high air.
It will be dark for the glider, lofted on weightlessness,
free to inscribe a line which leaves no trace,
floating toward nightfall, out of otherwhere.

# Umbilical

*—for Katherine, age eight*

It is not the first time
I have lost you,
betrayed you to the air:

your first cry
was witness enough.
Now you are goat-limbed,

shadow-eyed, and they wheel
you in fluorescent
silence down

a lengthening hall.
Neither of us protests.
You are swathed in sheets,

your body too long
and angular
to have curled in mine.

I let you fall
into the hands
of strangers, you grow

beyond me. In the waiting
room, I devour
a sandwich of

something limp, warm;
an article on
adoption; Balzac's

arias of debit
and credit. All time
sucks into void until

you land in time
stunned on the
recovery room bed.

How touch your other-
worldly skin? Blood drools
from your nostrils.

As your lids
quaver open and
pain hits, two

slow rivulets brim
and trek: from outer
space, you watch me.

Balzac thought money
wrenched the human
bond. It is our own

gravity draws us
down. I have
fallen light years

from my mother's
touch, yet now across
the waste of sheets

you ask me, "Hold
my hand." We are
in reach: and palm

to palm our life-
lines trace, for a
moment, a map.

# Song

A yellow coverlet
in the greenwood:
spread the corners wide to the dim, stoop-shouldered pines,
Let blank sky
be your canopy.
Fringe the bedspread with the wall of lapsing stones.
Here faith has cut
in upright granite
"Meet me in Heaven" at the grave of each child
lost the same year,
three, buried here,
a century ago. Roots and mosses hold
in the same bed
mother, daughter, dead
together, in one day. "Lord, remember the poor,"
their crumbling letters pray.
I turn away.
I shall meet you nowhere, in no transfigured hour.
On soft, matted soil
blueberry bushes crawl,
each separate berry a small, hot globe of tinctured sun.
Crushed on the tongue
it releases a pang
of flesh. Tender flesh, slipped from its skin,
preserves its blue heat
down my throat.

# The Twelfth Day

*—for Pam Cantor*

It is the twelfth day
The hero will not take food
He refuses wine   sleep   women

How can the body not spoil?
Dragged by chariot
gashed   smeared

in mud and horse droppings
Mutilate Mutilate
cries the hero's heart

as he lashes the horses
around and
around the tomb

If he can just
make his mark on this
corpse whose

beauty freshens
with each lunge
as though bathed

in balm   Even the gods
in gentle feast are
shocked: Is there no

shame? The hero has
no other life
He has taken

to heart a body
whose face vaulting
through gravel and blood

blends strangely
with the features
of that other

one: the Beloved
For this is
love: rigor

mortis in the
mortal grip
and never to let

go Achilles hoards
and defiles the dead
So what if heaven

and earth reverberate
*release*  So what
if Olympian

messages shoot through
cloudbanks sea
chambers ether

So what if everything
echoes the Father   *let go let*
*go*   This is Ancient

Poetry   It's supposed
to repeat
The living mangle the dead

after they mangle the living
It's formulaic
That's how we love   It's called

compulsion   Poetry can't
help itself
And no one has ever

explained how
light stabbed
the hero how he saw

in dawn salt mist
his Mother's face (she who
Was before words she

who would lose him)
Saw her but heard
words *Let him let*

*go*   Saw her and let
his fingers loosen
from that

suspended decay and
quietly
too quietly

turned away

# The Cost

That wasn't our baby
in the trashcan in the city zoo
someone else picked it out someone
else wrapped it in paper and dropped it in

>   Why do you sleep
>   with your back to me

Besides it's another city we don't
live there anymore

>   Because it's cold

Besides I collect
phrases these days not babies
*spartan clasp   jute finish   crotch island*

>   Last winter was colder
>   we lived by the Swedenborgian Institute
>   where you had your accident

Or that list of words from the summer in Florence
the essential list warm clues
like  *sausage   torture   bilge*  I knew
I'd need the rest of my life

but I lost it

>   The ice at the corner scared me

My hands soiled with news

That wasn't our baby

Virginity  elocution  electrocution
light sliding off the ailanthus spikes

It was another city

It was still breathing

The cost of empire is great and disturbing
the secret knowledge of philosophy

We weren't the ones

# Season Due

They are unforgiving and do not ask mercy, these last
of the season's flowers: chrysanthemums, brash
marigolds, fat sultan dahlias a-nod

    in rain. It is
    September. Pansy
    freaked with jet be

damned: it takes this radiant bitterness to
stand, to take the throb of sky, now sky
is cold, falls bodily, assaults. In tangled

    conclave, spiky-
    leaved, they
    wait. The news

is fatal. Leaf by leaf, petal
by petal, they brazen out this chill
which has felled already gentler flowers and herbs

    and now probes
    these veins for a last
    mortal volley of

cadmium orange, magenta, a last acrid flood
of perfume that will drift in the air here once more,
yet once more, when these stubborn flowers have died.

# STANLEY PLUMLY

## 1991

In his poems, Stanley Plumly brings a strong meditational quality to bear on lyricism's great themes: nature, death, dream, and the textures of actual objects. Trees and birds are in the poems, and so is the slow and powerful music of complex sentences. In his hands poems become bravely real and yet remain lyrically alert and very satisfying, and the result is an art of great steadiness and great depth.

—Donald Sheehan

# Naps

In a dream or fantasy I see my mother,
having put me down, leaning over me,
pulling the door shut twice, and if I rise
again, locking it. In school we were told
to put our heads down on the desks and think
of it as prayer or to lie on our left
sides on the floor, an inch between the pound
weight of the heart and passage of the earth.
We were told to listen to the silence.
not to talk, and breathe in slowly, slowly,
and pretend, if we had to, it was dark.
Already on our own we'd learned to study
out the window, to cogitate the tree
within the cloud, the long sunlit fingers
of the crow, and how to hold an object
in the mind and let it turn until it
turned the other life it wanted, the way
a doorknob with its facet-gaze of glass
becomes a diamond or a crystal,
and as you fall asleep, disintegrates,
snow in a paperweight. And now we were
intuiting sleeping the future,
the disconnected nights, the dawn-light wakings.
the shadow puzzles clouding up the windows,
the hardwood study table and a chair,
gravity's floor—a lifetime's worth of all
the afternoons we'd lose or lose part of
trying to recover what was lost. So
we'd use our hands and arms to blind the eyes,
and then the mind to separate ourselves.
Then wait the voice outside calling our return,

the same voice as the moment of instruction:
to lie down in the middle of the day,
dream fragmentary, dusk-enhancing dreams,
be the body-of-the-one-looked-upon,
come back to life, O startled, distant child.

# November 11, 1942–November 12, 1997

My friend's body walking toward me
down the Pullman passage of his hallway.
He's naked as if he's just risen
from a bath and forgotten what it is
he's supposed to do next. He looks cold,
candle-white, with a sort of sunburn
on his face, especially his mouth,
which is open on a vowel. And there
seems to be an almost visible vertical
line drawn through him, so that half
of him is taller, half in tow.
It must be afternoon, since the daylight
is going and the doorway behind him
disappearing. Now it's colder.
Now I realize that for the longest time
I've been waiting for him, and need
to think of something, and that
he's expecting it, the way silence
sometimes promises. Then suddenly
he's in front of me, and I can see
how damp he is, how anointed with oil,
how all the color's focused in the eyes,
how the coral of the brain shines through
the forehead. And though he doesn't say so,
because he never would, I'm sure he wants me
to hold him, say his name, make him warm.
But when I try he puts his hand inside
his heart and offers me the stone,
then the Armistice poppy, and then
the bowl of bright arterial blood.
And from where the scar is, where they

saved his life and failed, the umbilical
intestine, impurities and purities of kidneys
and the liver, the two lungs out of breath,
and breath itself, cupped till it runneth over.

# Piano

It must have been Lisa's voice
since she was waiting when we got there,
the bay doors barely open and her white
face running the bars along her stall.
Then Lisa brought her out into the hall
to brush her down in order to show
the wood sheen under the dust and how
the tension of the body, if she stood
still long enough, could make her look
like she was floating standing. And given
time, in the broken bird light falling
from the loft, she seemed to float,
nodding and letting her neck, a third
of all of her, bend to the floor,
where she swept, with little breaths,
each loose and useless piece until
she found the somewhere solid that
she wanted, striking the heavy air
to let us know, marking the place
to tell us, in a second, she could fly.
Her body had already started to shine,
but it was her blaze that gave her eyes
their depth against the touch and Lisa's
soft talk, that gave the eyes their depth.
And it was the eyes that sometimes flared
against the words. Lisa said she was wild
because she was young. And bored too
when she couldn't get out, yet never bored
the way some horses dance from side to side,
spelling their weight, pressing their radiant,
stalled foreheads into the walls, or the way

some horses disappear inside, having
drawn and redrawn circles. The barn was
full of the noise and silences of horses.
And filled with Lisa's voice in counter-
point: and Lisa's horse's stillnesses—
like love or what love's moment's stillness
really is, hands-high, and restless.

# Infidelity

The two-toned Olds swinging sideways out of
the drive, the bone-white gravel kicked up in
a shot, my mother in the deathseat half
out the door, the door half shut—she's being
pushed or wants to jump, I don't remember.
The Olds is two kinds of green, hand-painted,
and blows black smoke like a coal-oil fire. I'm
stunned and feel a wind, like a machine, pass
through me, through my heart and mouth; I'm standing
in a field not fifty feet away, the
wheel of the wind closing the distance.
Then suddenly the car stops and my mother
falls with nothing, nothing to break the fall...

One of those moments we give too much to,
like the moment of acknowledgment of
betrayal, when the one who's faithless has
nothing more to say and the silence is
terrifying since you must choose between
one or the other emptiness. I know
my mother's face was covered black with blood
and that when she rose she too said nothing.
Language is a darkness pulled out of us.
But I screamed that day she was almost killed,
whether I wept or ran or threw a stone,
or stood stone-still, choosing at last between
parents, one of whom was driving away.

# Sickle

Sharper than the scythe, which, like the ladder
and the boards I couldn't lift, was long.
And quicker, since it was smaller,
and, swung in an arc, would sing.
I was the age of Latin in school, *mollis*
for mullein, the flannel of whose leaf
girls would rouge their Quaker cheeks with,
for whom vanity, even beauty, was a wildflower.
Weeds were waste, like the milkweed's semen milk,
and this was work that I could do, through
afternoons the sun would drive
your bare head into your shoulders.
Then a need for salt and the spilling
of some blood, blisters and exhaustion,
lacerate missed chances, biblical water poured—
carrot lace and goldenrod swept
to the ground like harvest, star-thorn
Canada thistle cut to the rose at the root.
I used the sickle because the scythe
was too much weight, and because death's
instrument, on the shoulder of the monk's head's
hood-and-mantle, looked too much like it.
You wanted, when you were finished, a field.

# Strays

They'd show up at evening, with the change
of light, between a long day and supper,
close to the road or edge of the yard,
heads low, half starved, but quick as crows.
If you fed them, left meat scraps out at night,
they'd come back hungrier, and if you didn't,
if you ignored them or threw stones, they'd
simply back away, wary, starving, waiting
for dark in order to raid the smoking ashes
of the garbage, sometimes alone or in pairs,
sometimes in cerberus three-headed numbers.
They seemed almost to live somewhere, and near,
as certain of their ground as neighbors.

Serious neighbors shot them or tried poison,
while my father went to gather what he could
into the cowbed of his truck to be ferried.
Dogs that year were let out everywhere,
mongrels, pets, freak accidents, some with
mange or worse, the year of the holiday
death counts, the year somebody driving fast
blind-sided one in front of the house,
sent it flying all at once over the car:
it rose where it fell, where nobody wanted
to touch it since it acted still alive,
its puffed pink tongue lolling in its blood,
its canine neutral eye rolled over white.

We'd seen death before, and death brought back
to life, the spirit arm or leg of what was
missing from a boy, the mouth of the polio

friend breathing again, the ice of her face
on fire. But this was filled, unbroken flesh
continuous, the matted hair and open sores
unchanged. Somebody said, and I wished I'd
said it, let's find a place and bury it,
which nobody wanted to do, for fear of rabies
or a dog's disease. Finally one of the fathers
took a hind in each warm hand and dragged
the animal dead weight over to the shoulder
where serious crows and flies resurrect.

# Reading with the Poets

Whitman among the wounded, at the bedside,
kissing the blood off boys' faces, sometimes stilled
faces, writing their letters, writing the letters
home, saying, sometimes, the white prayers, helping,
sometimes, with the bodies or holding the bodies
down. The boy with the scar that cuts through his speech,
who's followed us here to the Elizabeth
Zane Memorial and Cemetery, wants
to speak nevertheless on the Civil War's
stone-scarred rows of dead and the battle here
just outside of Wheeling equal in death to
Gettysburg because no doctor between the war
and Pittsburgh was possible. Boys dressed like men

and men would gangrene first before the shock of
the saw and scalpel. Three days between this part
of the Ohio River and Pittsburgh. He
knows, he is here since then a child of history
and knows Elizabeth Zane saved all she could.
Keats all his wounded life wanted to be a healer,
which he was, once at his mother's bedside, failed,
once at his brother's, failed. Whitman in Washington
failed: how many nights on the watch and it broke
him, all those broken boys, all those bodies blessed
into the abyss. Now the poem for Lincoln,
now the boy with the scar almost singing, now

the oldest surviving poet of the war
reading one good line, then another, then
the song of the hermit thrush from the ground cover.
Lincoln's long black brooding body sailed in a train,

a train at the speed of the wind blossoming,
filling and unfilling the trees, a man's slow
running. Whitman had nowhere to go, so I
leave thee lilac with heart-shaped leaves, he says at
last, and went to the other side with the corpses,
myriads of them, soldiers' white skeletons,
far enough into the heart of the flower
that none of them suffered, none of them grieved, though
the living had built whole cities around them.

Keats at his medical lectures drew flowers.
Not from indifference, not from his elegance:
his interest couldn't bear the remarkable
screams of the demonstrations. He sat there, still
a boy, already broken, looking into the living
body, listening to the arias of the spirit
climbing. So the boy at the graves of the Union
singing, saying his vision, seeing the bodies
broken into the ground. Now the poem for Lincoln.
Now the oldest surviving poet still alive
weaving with the audience that gossamer,
that thread of the thing we find in the voice again.
Now in the night our faces kissed by the heater.

# ROBERT CORDING

## 1992

In his poems, Robert Cording realizes what the ancient Hebrew Psalmists knew: that all grace has weight—is heavy—because all our love is slipping through our fingers "so unaccountably fast," as Cording says in one of his poems. But what could (and does) so easily result in resentment manifests, instead, in his poems as that profound psalmic condition called waiting; "My soul waits for the Lord," says Psalm 130, which Cording quotes. In this waiting, this attentive, alert waiting, Robert Cording's poems focus all our fears and resentments in perfect psalmic forgiveness.

—Donald Sheehan

# White Mountains

At times they nested above us,
Hugely fixed in silent considerings,
Shadow lakes pooled along their sides
As rafts of clouds passed across
The sun. At other times, weightless
As breath, chameleon-like,
They could take the color of rain
And vanish behind a scrim of cloud.
Always expected and always strange—
How, staying in exactly the same place,
The mountains were continually leaving,
Day after day, the gray rock
At the peaks gradually darkening
To smokey blue, becoming unmoored
In the Chinese-misted drift of evening.
All that summer as we read or turned
From books, as we stood on the porch
Or moved through our daily tasks
Toward each other, they bridged
Our pleasure and our pain. In the end
We came to believe the mountains
Brought us to some acceptance
Of loss—if only that their high,
Indifferent, ceaseless passing away
Became our only home, their shadow
Line of smoke like the smoke
From the dozen houses on Ridge Road
Where, talking in whispers before sleep,
We spoke of what was still to be done,
The day gone by so unaccountably fast.

# Sam Cooke: *Touch the Hem of His Garment*

As if he cannot help himself
from adding up what's lost to the good times
   so difficult to have in this world,

   Cooke's throaty voice warbles
up out of his reed-thin, man-child body,
   half-balm, half aching need,

   his trademark whoa-ooh-oh-oh-oh
lingered over, drawn out until it hangs in air,
   honey-tongued, heavenly, fragile

   as consolation. I'm listening
to a 1956 recording, and Cooke, twenty-five,
   has already discovered his gift

   for making women tremble
and shake with the spirit in church aisles.
   He's retelling the Gospel story

   of a woman who wants only
to touch the hem of Christ's robe, a song
   that will sell twenty-five thousand copies,

   propel Cooke into a gospel star,
and begin the long chain of small decisions
   that ends with a bullet in his lungs.

   Still eight years away—
the $3-and-up motel, the hooker charging
   assault, Cooke's cherry red Ferrari

purring in the parking lot
as he slumps to the floor, naked save for
    an overcoat and one expensive shoe—

    but I can't keep from hearing
the urgency in his voice as the woman, pushed
    by the terror of self-recognition,

    her flesh dying from the inside
out, staggers through the crowd around Jesus,
    and, with only the slightest brush

    of her fingers, touches
his robe, believing it will make her whole.
    *Who has touched me?* Jesus asks,

    and Cooke sings, *It was I-I-I,*
extending the moment in his clear, sustained
    yodel, pulling us into the miracle

    of how, after night-long drifts
from bar to bar, the slur of zippers and
    whiskeyed words dimming the nameless

    landscapes of a hundred
identical blackened factories stuck between
    billboards and railway bridges,

    after a week of days piling
one on another like dirty laundry, Sunday arrives,
    and everyone rises and testifies

    and sways under the wings
of notes that swoop and glide and make us whole,
    if only for the duration of the song.

# Against Consolation

The lecturer is talking
about Weil's essay on "Detachment."
    The scent of lilacs
intoxicates the air inside the room,

    cut branches brought in
to represent the flowering outside,
    spring flaring up
again like those beliefs, I imagine,

    Weil warns against—
*beliefs which fill up voids and sweeten*
    *what is bitter.* A thousand
miles from here, you have given up

    belief in the providential
ordering of events. No proverb sweetens
    your suffering. What endures
is your bewilderment—the freakish

    wheel of that truck
breaking off and hurtling through
    the sunlit air, not enough
time to say *Look out* or even *Shit,*

    before it struck
your car, one of hundreds lined up
    in rush-hour traffic
on the other side of the highway.

You told me, the more
you think, the less you understand.
    You can't explain
the roof caved in all around you,

    your two friends buried
under metal, and you, who sat alongside
    them, untouched.
Home from the hospital, your friends

    dead, you went to
the kitchen, and everything, you said,
    was just as you left it,
as if the accident were only an interruption

    in daily life, a tornado
that leaves a kitchen table set for dinner.
    *The contradictions the mind*
*comes up against—these are the only realities:*

    *they are the criterion*
*of the real.* Weil again, who believes,
    we come to know
our *radical contingency* only through

    such contradictions.
We must suffer them unconsoled.
    "Let the accident go,"
your friends tell you, "Don't hold on"—

    what we say, I fear,
to rid ourselves of the pain we feel
    when your pain closes
in on us. It's late in the afternoon

and the rustling
of feet and papers has begun. I look out
   the window—a gusty wind
polishes the morning's rain-washed glass

   of air, and the late sun
lavishes each new green with its shine.
   I'd like to dismiss Weil's
haunted, unnerving life as my colleague

   quickly does, the lecture
ended: "Brilliant, but crazy." Anorexic,
   psychotic, suicidal. Labels
that fit, I suppose, and yet I cannot deny

   the stark attraction
of her words. *Stay with your suffering,*
   I've heard her say
over and over today, always the extremist.

   The last time I saw you,
I knew you lived at the border of what is
   bearable, that you'd seen
the skeleton underneath all your thought,

   everything stripped
of sense or summation; you knew
   your friends' deaths
would make no more sense in time

   and you would have
to live in that knowledge—no, not
   *knowledge,* the word
itself a kind of consolation, but the void

Weil speaks of,
where you cannot escape the skewed
     wheel of a truck, the blood
on your hands, the voice you still have

     that calls out, *O God, no,*
the scent of lilacs that pierce the air
     each spring for no cause,
beautifully innocent of meaning.

# Self-Portrait

So strongly present, enclosed
in familiar features: all you
ever see, your self, unreal
to the Buddhist monk, but
something you cannot get rid of.

Inconceivable, this face, yours
just once to wear, that says, *You
can go this far and no further.*
That grins, self-mockingly,
when you try to reach with words'

tenuous liaisons what you believe
words do not invent.
Your petitions repeat themselves,
endlessly trying to get it right,
but still you hear only

your own voice, your will
never strong enough
to will nothing. So here
you are, fleshed out in features
that tell the same old story

year after year, the end
just beginning to make itself
clear in the boney ridges
rising to the surface
of your cheeks, in the deep

holes into which your eyes
stare, and sink, an emptiness
asking, *What have you ever seen*
*beyond the point of vanishing*
*to which we have brought you?*

# Between Worlds

At the room's threshold you paused
as if caught by the stillness at the heart
of grief's sheer drop and, like Vermeer's
woman holding up her empty scales
in the window's light, you held the room's
remote self-containment: the sadness
of failing light at the windows; the few
things no longer his—a ring of keys,
a wallet, some prayer books; the lamp
and clock on the side table; the rented
hospital bed, stripped now, that waited
like a bed in some halfway house
between worlds where the dying sift
through the last certainties that prop up
their lives, and then are gone, leaving
the dumbstruck living to weigh
an unthinkable life, a death, an empty room.

# Gratitude

In his prison letters, Bonhoeffer is thankful
for a hairbrush, for a pipe and tobacco,
for cigarettes and Schelling's *Morals* Vol. II.
Thankful for stain remover, laxatives,
collar studs, bottled fruit and cooling salts.
For his Bible and hymns praising what is
fearful, which he sings, pacing in circles
for exercise, to his cell walls where he's hung
a reproduction of Durer's *Apocalypse*.
He's thankful for letters from his parents
and friends that lead him back home,
and for the pain of memory's arrival,
his orderly room of books and prints too far
from the nightly sobs of a prisoner
in the next cell whom Bonhoeffer does not know
how to comfort, though he believes religion
begins with a neighbor who is within reach.
He's thankful for the few hours outside
in the prison yard, and for the half-strangled
laughter between inmates as they sit together
under a chestnut tree. He's thankful even
for a small ant hill, and for the ants that are
all purpose and clear decision. For the two
lime trees that mumble audibly with the workings
of bees in June and especially for the warm
laying on of sun that tells him he's a man
created of earth and not of air and thoughts.
He's thankful for minutes when his reading
and writing fill up the emptiness of time,
and for those moments when he sees himself
as a small figure in a vast, unrolling scroll,

though mostly he looks out over the plains
of ignorance inside himself. And for that,
too, he's thankful: for the self who asks,
*Who am I?*—the man who steps cheerfully
from this cell and speaks easily to his jailers,
or the man who is restless and trembling
with anger and despair as cities burn and Jews
are herded into railroad cars—can
without an answer, say finally, *I am thine,*
to a God who lives each day,
as Bonhoeffer must, in the knowledge
of what has been done, is still being done,
his gift a refusal to leave his suffering, for which,
even as the rope is placed around his neck
and pulled tight, Bonhoeffer is utterly grateful.

# SHARON BRYAN

## 1993

I n her poems, Sharon Bryan employs a grace of syntax. Hers is one of the most interesting and beautiful voices we have. It's a voice that is astonishingly fresh. She engages issues of shelter, of home, and its losses—losses grave and irrevocable. Like Robert Frost's poems, her poems know the saving shrewdness of art, the shrewdness that comes only from strong lyric grace.

—Donald Sheehan

# Big Sheep Knocks You About

*I've shorn over two hunn'ert in a day,*
*but big sheep knocks you about. I used*
*to go mad at it, twisting and turning*
*all night. Couldn't sleep after a rough*
*day with the sheep.*

### 1

In town, in the foodshop, men are making sandwiches,
cutting bread, cutting meat, cutting onions. The essence of
all these mixes with grease on their aprons, and blood from
cut thumbs. When they wipe their faces at night it is to
remember the day. They are good at what they do, and
beautiful to watch: silver, flesh, silver, flesh.

### 2

In the foodshop a boy with thick 15-year-old hands is trying
to help, but the bread breaks and mixes with the bits of meat
and sauce, though his hands move after theirs the way a
poem is said to be after the Greek. They laugh, knowing
they can teach him, and his hands go on rising and falling
like lungs.

The boy's hands on himself at night are surer, though
hurrying makes them clumsy, and shame that they should be
graceful at what they're doing. When his hands move over a
girl's body they are lost to him, so he dreams of sea skates
brushing coral. Of killing someone without meaning to. His
mother settling over his face like a pillow. Home he makes
himself come twice before he can sleep.

3

And the boy's father dreams of England and Nettie leaning
fat against the wall with nothing on but her stockings, saying
Roll me 'round again, dearie. You know how I like it.


4

One stinks of blood and grease, flinty dead cells of hooves.
Two always face each other in profile, in the Greek curls of
    their horns and snouts and lips.
Three form a wedge that comes to a point just out of sight
    behind you.
Four run earnestly bunched in the same direction.
Five are not a team. They are dumb, they jostle and bump.
Six keep to themselves, just, in the crowd, avoiding each
    other with the grace of passivity.
Seven is used only by people.
Eight is not the seeds of dissent, these are sheep.
Nine is not the beginnings of mathematics.
Ten is a congregation with no preacher.
So is eleven.
Twelve has an unbreachable shape of its own, like a fertilized
    egg,
but at thirteen the edges begin to buckle and scallop,
at fourteen the sheep mill and mutter, and the dust rises
    to their ankles.
Beyond this the only shape comes from fences and short
    grass, humans circling, sheep circling.


5

In all the jokes it's the men who fuck sheep, drawn to the
puckery assholes, and it's perfectly natural that Black Bart's

girl is the wooliest. But when a woman dreams of sheep, it's of the weight and thickness, its penis stiff along the sheep's belly, steamy in the cold, its horns spiraling invisibly in the dark.

The story of Leda was begun by a woman: . . . settling over me, like the sky, and making my tongue swell in my mouth . . . And ended by a man: . . . a bird, with air in its bones. With eyes that see two things instead of one.

# Abracadabra

A man was dying—
slowly at first, he said,
then the river he was riding

divided, he went one way
everyone else the other,
soon for him there was nothing

but darkness and pain—
he was adamant about that,
no welcoming light—

then he began to fall, it was
the feeling that yanks us back
from the edge of sleep,

but not him, not this time,
he kept on dropping
for what seemed like forever,

just the twist in the pit
of his stomach to tell him
he was still alive,

still falling, until finally
there was something
else, a little tickle

at the back of his mind,
a notion that might slow him
if only he could get hold of it—

what he needed was a word,
a particular word,
but none came to him

for another long time,
then one began to take shape—
the pain was even worse

at first, but he wasn't falling
as fast, and then at long long last
he stopped:

this was just the beginning
of coming back, he had to feel
his way up the well

he seemed to have fallen down,
lifting his entire weight
every inch with his fingertips,

it took hours or days,
he couldn't tell which and the word
that had made it possible

was *hope*—when he came to that part
of the story, we were embarrassed,
we looked at each other and not

at him: it was too obvious, too
sentimental, a sign of weakness
in a strong man, we chalked it up

to his illness—but what did he care
about irony and narrative
distance? He knew he'd sat up

in bed, asked for his shoes,
and taken his son to a movie,
*Conan the Barbarian.*

He lived another year
on that one word plucked
from thin air.

*—for Richard Blessing*

# What I Want

I don't see any wolves at first,
they're so limply asleep
in the dry grass. Then one lifts

its head, teeters to its feet,
turns its snout in our direction
for a long minute before the strings

let go and he refolds himself
to sleep. Now I know what to look for
I count six bags of bones

you've come to the zoo to say
good-bye to, I've come to say good-bye
to you, and I want the wolves you love

to rise and press their noses to the fence.
As if they could absolve me
of anything. They are oblivious

to the weight of what I want,
what you want. You carry yourself
as if you might break, while I praise

the reticulate giraffe
because it has no lessons to teach us.
Not one beautiful animal in here

wants to hold us, except as food.
Because I don't know what to say to you,
I've never been so tired of words.

And so tired of my body, which will not
hold you any more than the wolves
will come forward to ease your going.

# One Basket

Chance and ignorance give us a little
grace period. We do not have to choose
which redolent eggs will be lost,
which pause to become our children
spelling themselves out. *Elizabeth*
I might have called a daughter. How slow

I am to give her up altogether, how slow
to get the tone right, not a little
sentimental: dear Elizabeth.
I give her red hair, blue eyes, choose
her disposition. Imaginary children
are constant companions, like all lost

opportunities. I have willfully lost
myself in thoughts of angels, turning slow
on luminous pins. As our own children,
some of us tend ourselves like little
gardens. I do not want to say I choose
this, I turn my back on Elizabeth.

*Anything is possible.* Elizabeth—
not true. Those who believe it are lost.
It is not even that I must choose
between you and my work—you are slow!—
but I must unname you, hold you a little
to the light, see through you. No children,

no births, no pregnancies. Real children
can't wait for our next lives. Elizabeth
lulls me by demanding so little.

When Jacob wrestled the angel he lost
false fears and was blessed. The unbearably slow
motion of that battle forced him to choose

one life incessantly all night, to choose
this one. Again, this one. I have no children.
Too easy: I will not have. Knowledge is slow
to collapse on itself. Elizabeth,
may your half-truths unwind in the earth, be lost
in that acid babble signifying little.

When we are children we long to be lost
briefly. Elizabeth is a slow
name to unthread. I choose my way a little.

# The Same River Twice

I am leaving, I put on my earring,
shape of a silver fish.
I am leaving, I put on my red hat
with no flower.
I pull on one sock in a hurry.
I wash my face wearing my hat.
I button my blouse
over my breasts. I unbutton one button,
but you are by the window.
Half the irises are blooming.
I look in my purse and in my pocket
and in my hand. What can I do
without? My shoes are ahead of me,
pointing out the door.

# Bad News

A friend is ill, a cousin dead:
I know what to say when I call
and your voice, like matchlight,
summons your face. I almost know,
from your silences, what not to say.

This is safe ground, the king's X
of childhood games, charmed circle,
crossed fingers, time out. The tenuous
terms of estrangement. Wires thin
as human hair suspend the universe

we were once the center of. I can't
remember if light travels forever
with nothing to stop it, or if
the dark drinks it as the earth does
a river. I pause mid-sentence.

Now even loss is something
we no longer have in common.
You say you hope next time the news
will be better. I stand on one foot—
because, like the bird in the joke,

I'd fall down if I didn't.
In the future no news will be
good enough, the road we've abandoned
a faint derangement of the landscape,
visible only from the air.

# MARK HALLIDAY

## 1994

I n his poems, Mark Halliday engages as his subject the excitement of mental energy, an excitement that's released by giving the mind free rein to see itself as it sees the world and listens to the world. One consequence of this, of course, is comedy. With this amount of perception, of course our lives appear silly. But what is very rare in these poems' comedy is their compassion. Mark Halliday has the capacity to see and experience even the silliness as a blessing. He gives us an art of intelligent joy.

—Donald Sheehan

# Franconia

Mem-mem we remem-mem we
that house, we remember those rooms, those shadowed
rooms: there was a dampness; the dampness offered
a comfortably inescapable metaphor for the trapped
innerness of mind, so we sat and stood and moved in
the metaphor, shadows of that.
Mem-mem...
                    That house,
the white slats of the house were pale gray in
the afternoon of then. Along the dusty road passed
an old car pale green rather fast along in the lives of
neighbors not met. In the sloping yard there was
that grass of course that grass there and a few
tufted-up rocks near the barn, the restored barn.
Then then then then. Restored, to be restored—
sound of the latch
                          on the barn door, sound of
the screen door on the side porch
there there there then and the spiders and the earwigs,
earwigs of reality yes in the bathtub as we recall
in that small house afloat in afternoon of then.
Tall lilies of the past they were orange I think grew
as we tried to grow too but more vaguely than the lilies
all along in front of the long front porch long long
front porch of that house—all this occurring

in the then afternoon waiting for elegy;
that house—remem—white slats
white slats never quite seen? nor the dense grass
nor the lilies ever quite seen? To be restored
sitting in a damp shady room turning pages of

a black notebook we were happy enough while still
missing most of each day; is there another way?
Sound of the latch—

# This Man

This man moved through a tunnel and a garden
and a maze of alleys and through a forest he moved.
He glanced and he went. Carefully he glanced.
The geese overflew him. He had the one problem
and two other problems. Useful machines whickered
and shook and quit. So this man negotiated.
Through alleys and lanes he moved
as the first problem clanged like a load of tins.
But he made an odd choice and the odd choice tossed
that problem to the side. So the man breathed
and he moved farther. Boxes on both sides made shadows.
To the south there was gunfire. The sun was dumb.
This man then moved farther, around the white warehouse
and between the scabbed villas. A radio on a roof said
he meant nothing in the long run. But this man was moving

and he was standing and he was breathing
separate from dirt. His head clamored like a free city.
Then came the problem with brass buckles behind
ten folds of leather. Across the bridge came fear.
But this man found black wires and he made two locks,
two pinches, two hinges and two twirled ingressions,
and he made two braces. Carefully he glanced and he watched
until change flashed like tossed glass. Then this man
breathed and he wrote a note. He climbed on a train.
The smoke billowed high toward infinity above the train.
The man tilted his hat and he ranged stacks upon a table

when the third problem spilled black fluid on his shoes.
It formed beads and then balls banging in a chilly hail
until his hat bounced out a window. So this man

went on with no hat. He said seven words over and over
as rock bluffs plunked upon his hips and elbows.
Gray friction was all around. There was smutched clogged
flattening air from dumb clouds and no person was close
no person close no one finally close next to him.
But he swiveled, he sculpted another odd choice
(too peculiar from the vantage of chromey towers)
and blue dots became streaks and then a blue street.

So this man was still not dirt
and he breathed and thought, and went.

# Unconversation

Among people
you sort of half-step toward me but then a faltering
    prevails
due to tiny transparent bats that bounce off our
    cheekbones:
they are the conversations that probably won't happen.
I look down. I look into my tepid coffee.
You glance at my ear;
I glance at your eyebrow;
you pass through space
between wool shoulders and we are relieved
and we are sad. Pelted by tiny glass bats
we wobble sideways around the noisy room.
This room is so full of people, folks, people,
les hommes et les femmes—
les hommes et les femmes les hommes et les femmes—
oy. At moments I seem to love
the way they stand and the way they tilt their heads.
However, they are manifestly *too much*.
The male gaze, the female gaze, the person-as-such gaze,
I want a helmet with a visor!
I look at a light on a building across the street
and I'm grateful for the distance between me and this light.
The light is small and cold and far and so
it is safe and safe is good, with a type of beauty,
it is the Convenient Transcendent.
You are down the hall. I think I hear your voice
saying something something father or farther,
something something mixing them or Michigan,
Something something Thomas Edison or Tommy's medicine.
Your voice is a rag of a flag waving from a schooner near

      the horizon,
it is a flaring of the string section in the symphony of
what has occurred elsewhere, for other people,
in the green field of the conversations that do happen.
I accept this
with a kind of dry creaking of the skin on my face
which seems to me the symptom of my courage
in coping with fatigue. People
are often attractive but *always* tiring
so it's no wonder the room is filling up
with the conversations that will not have happened.
Friendly questions and serious answers never uttered
are flicking against the furniture, flying caterpillars
that will never be life-affirming Lepidoptera.
Wait, didn't I say they were glass bats?  But
what's the difference if no one is listening?
And I have had enough of metaphor now.
It is sticky and gummy like—like humanness!
This gray crust tufting my eyebrows and casting a shadow
across the dry creaking of my face—
it is the detritus from the smashing of tiny creatures
made of untalked talk!  Humanity—it is humanity
that has tufted me with gray crust.
Oh I look down.
Oh my far cold light.
I shall seek my bed.
Good night.

But tomorrow—well, tomorrow I might run into you.
In some bookstore, some bakery—
it could be in Greenfield, Massachusetts—
weird things happen—-we might suddenly get
weirdly HUMAN together—uncrusted.
Okay?  Tomorrow.  Talk to you later, person.

# Sourdough

If abruptly it appears that we're all just sandwiches
transformed by chewing, all just healthy organisms
walking our little walks toward auspicious mating,
writing our plotty little novels about
progress toward mating, discussing some shoddy glittered
movie about little bumps on the path toward
auspicious mating, all eating our thick sandwiches
on sourdough bread and floating toward cancer
not now but ten years later or thirty-five years later
on the ticking schedule for well-shod well-shirted
healthy blah—
temporary skin coating temporary flesh
all saying "a positive outlook" and
"reassess the priorities" amid the sandwich—

the generality is what pulls toward void.
Quickly identify the particular restaurant,
the partic. street, a partic. funny scene
in that shoddy movie, drink a Lynchburg Lemonade
and quote something from page 77 of a partic. book
and say I *love* that, actually.

# Schnetzer Day

This amazing fine song comes on the radio
the day after my death,
it's Greenie Schnetzer and the Generous Glands
singing "Defrocked Bishop of Love" and it is gorgeous.
The song combines the feel of "Get a Job" by the Silhouettes
with the sexy speed of "Roadrunner" as performed by
Joan Jett and the Blackhearts, and someone hears it
and realizes all this. Less than a day has passed
since my demise, and someone feeling comfortable
in a soft pair of old jeans suddenly remembers
the calm weary face of his mother, or sister,
a few weeks before she died of cancer, and also
sees back to his father one sad Christmas
saying "This Bulgarian wine is surprisingly good"
and has a sense of how people keep trying. Also
someone wearing an old ₁erringbone jacket in a hallway
sings "Gypsy gal" softly and it means a great deal.
And around a corner comes a certain potential romantic partner
and says "Lunch?"
                    Meanwhile I'm dead.
In a school gym some guy makes an absurd hook shot
from downtown, nothing but net, with his favorite Susan watching.
And a person wearing a Portland Sea Dogs cap
finishes a poem by rhyming "tyro" with "Cairo"
and places warm forehead against a cool pane of glass.
And there's more, involving funny children and T. S. Eliot,
but already it seems obvious that my death is a bad mistake—
just think of Greenie Schnetzer!—
and I guess in fact I'd better live forever.

# Why Must We Write?

Because of the wave. And because
the streets radiate into three more neighborhoods
than we have even ever heard of, in our own town!
Because everything just left. And because
those people at the table laughed
when we didn't know about tequila or Nietzsche.
Then came the dead streetlamp.
Hence we must write. Also because

for 3 percent of us there will be
fabulous jobs in which mainly we can just read books
for thirty years and talk about the ones we've read
and the ones we haven't read. Also
for another 14 percent of us there will be
decent tolerable jobs permitting in rather brownish ways
a tolerable amount of the fine wordy dreaming
we will die saying we need more of.
If we write, if we write a great deal, if
we stay home from the video store and write more
then we really might get into the 14 percent
and even, who knows, even who knows eventually into
the blessed 3 percent whose names we try to remember.
To remember because otherwise there is only the forgetting
which is so common, so K-Mart,
so have-another-basket-of-ribs-and-die. So thus

we write. Because of the wave.
Because the castle is of sand. Because
the pressure is immense of taxis and taxes and toxic waste
and the Internet and five ways to maximize investment growth
and low-fat high-health trim-line budget-conscious

workout plans
and the thing that surpasses your current audio system

and because Patricia turned away as if bored.
In the room where people were getting their coats,
seeming so pleased with their coats
and mentioning favorite sectors of northern Italy,
Patricia turned away from me as if I was boring to her.
Wait till she sees my books! But also because

the little boy uncombed and scuffing
at sunset on the Amtrak platform in Bridgeport
looked strangely familiar and seemed to matter
terribly somehow and we did not speak to him.

# LUCI TAPAHONSO

## 1995

In her poems, Luci Tapahonso reveals the language and culture of an ancient people, intact and lived with simplicity and depth in a time and place profoundly hostile to all such historical intactness. One might expect that this ancient language and culture would need, above all, to be protected, sheltered, even hidden from the violent destroyers. Yet here is the miracle of Luci Tapahonso's poems: as they reveal the Navajo Nation, the poems possess this Nation's aliveness precisely by giving it to us. "See," her poems say (echoing John Keats), "here is my hand, I hold it towards you."

—Donald Sheehan

# A Whispered Chant of Loneliness

I awaken at 1:20 then sit in the dark living room.
Numbers click time on silent machines.
Everyone sleeps.
Down the street, music hums, someone laughs.
                    It floats: an unseen breath through the window screen.

        My father uses a cane and each day,
        he walks outside to sit in the southern sunlight.
        He reads the *National Geographic*, the *Daily Times*,
        and the *Gallup Independent*.
        He remembers all this and minute details of my life.
        Sometimes he tells my children smiling.

        His voice is an old rhythm of my childhood.
        He read us stories of Goldilocks and The Three Bears
        and a pig named "Greased Lightning."
        He held us close, sang throaty songs,
        and danced Yei bicheii in the kitchen.

        His voice is a steady presence in my mothering.
        Some years ago, he handed me a cup of coffee
        and told me that sometimes leaving a relationship
        was an act of abiding strength.
        He told me that my children would not be sad always.

        Tonight I want to hear him speak to me.
        He thinks I look like my mother did at 38.
        Just last week, I heard her laughter in my own.

This winter, my life is a series of motions.
Each morning, I get up and shower,

have breakfast for my daughter,
drink a cup of coffee, then warm the car for five minutes.

I continue. My days: an undercurrent of fear,
                an outpouring of love,
                  a whispered chant of loneliness.

# DAVID GRAHAM

## 1996

In considering David Graham's poems, we become aware of a vexing issue in describing poetry: we say of a poet, he is "merely graceful" or "merely intelligent"—but how very difficult it is to achieve grace and lucidity in our poems. David Graham achieves both in his poems—the real and right thing—something I want to call moral goodness, a quality that has more to do with enchantment than with ethics, and everything to do with song. The poems are generous, open, good-hearted, and (Aristotle's beautiful word in *Ethics*) great-souled. We say of a young poet, "He has much to learn." Of David Graham, I want to say, "He has so much to teach."

—Donald Sheehan

# Summons

The whole time we slept
raccoons stretched and batted
like dreamy cats on our roof.
Not five feet from our pillow
they gamboled, scritching the shingles,
brushing our windowscreen
with ardent fur. Dew-christened
aerialists, they might as well
have sprouted from the dark
like sudden mushrooms, or dropped
on our porch roof by the moon.

I had no need to see
by their ironic masks
what they might think of our married
slumber, side by side like chunks
of firewood, while in the bright
spring air and moonwash this pair
frisked for their own cloudy benefit.

By the time the dog roused us
with his strangled growl, on point
before our common window,
I knew without a glance
what my flashlight would reveal
hissing and humming near at hand—
what else but love itself
somersaulting its antic way
all over our mended roof?

# Honeymoon Island

*—Florida 1997*

Shell-white northerners in January sun,
we follow bird tracks farther and farther
from the woods path, drunk on greenhouse air,
squinting even with shades as we round a curve
and meet the Gulf: a flock of ibises
in the shallows like a stiff cocktail party,
egret alert just over the next low dune.
Osprey nesting in dead firs at our back,
a turtle on pause in the white sand just ahead.

An hour at most we've stolen
between obligations, lucky to find
this profuse and garish dream island,
strange spiky blooms in the freighted air.
Sun nearly bleaches all thought away,
easing blizzard and black ice, thawing
stopped pipes and dammed gutters.
We murmur new surprise at every fresh
knife edge of greenery, each houseplant
somehow looming taller than a house.

I wish I could say now I take your hand
and speak my heart, but we just continue
ambling our languid sky-and-sand circle
of this hothouse island, soon enough arriving
back at our rental car, chatting of night plans,
the cancer even then busy blooming in your chest.

# Eviction Elegy

*—to the memory of Shirley Anders, 1934–1994*

Never to read a new poem of yours stuttering across the page
in your comma-heavy way with first drafts, as though
each sentence could end at any time, and maybe ought to,

never again your slightly over-enunciating voice
snaking its way through my own syntax, exploding
with a "Mercy me!" or "I'll be a *who*-knows-what!"

at some casual turn of mine, or nailing a phony adjective
with stately relish, followed by your predictable eruption:
"Pay no *attention* to me in my neurotic nit-pickiness!"

—I'm picking through my basket of *nevers*, bruised fruit
I doubt you'd want to trifle with, my friend. If I'd tried
to call you in those last weeks I would have known

your phone disconnected; if I'd knocked on your door
I would have seen the Eviction notice ignored and curling.
But I was already evicted from your strange life,

blinded as ever in the spotlight of your absolute concern.
Your last poem I saw was "For Joan in a Difficult Season,"
gazing with love and cool clear eye at your sister,

"stunned after the fire and after the diagnosis." Stunned
is right, I guess: I always took you to be as tough as you looked.
I never knew the days, the weeks it sometimes took

to ready your face for public view. I wrote you a fan letter
the year we both published our first books, remember?
You never replied to my gush, but when two years later

you settled nearby, we struck up that on-the-fly friendship
of writing teachers: a conference here, a dinner there,
and three or four times a year, our drafts spread out for correction

and praise. I never told you: I knew exactly what that poem
to your sister was truly about, knew and could not say,
respecting your privacy unto death. Now it's almost

a year since you took that last bus home, and you lie
(if anywhere) in those fog-layered mountains you loved
and left for our marshes and prairie flats. By now

you've fed the daffodils and redbud, forsythia
like electric shouts along the spring hillsides. I know
if you were here you would have changed the subject

long ago, so I'll leave you in as much peace as I can muster.
I'll leave you now as I left you then to go so strangely solo
into your own difficult season, crab nipping your empty womb

as who-knows-what bit down on your mind.

# Vietnam Memorial

Black wing wedged in civic earth,
      less gravestone
than plane crash, its only glory

the black sun it gives back
      to us, our frowns
swimming the polish and glare.

Like a river fluent under ice,
      it moves and doesn't,
Washington T. Douglass and Irwin

Ledoux, Federico Vasquez, Paul Robert Kort.
      Sorrow hypnotizes
like water, the years sloping

down to deeper death, name by name
      chiseled clean.
There's room at the tapering tips

for a few dozen more to sink
      into midnight rock
—unlikely, but who's ruling it out?

We taper, too, rising finally
      as the mourners
we are. Moving slowly from that

angled center, quieted by the stone's
      surprising size,
we have nothing to say but the few names

lodged in memory as a stone is held
in sand. Randolph
Cerrone. Martin Jackson, Jr.  John Pass.

# Homage to Sadie Bosheers

Sadie, you gave me this shirt on my back,
tested my wayward seams and tugged my buttons
long before I knew I would clothe myself
in your care. So I wanted you to know
I keep your cryptic message, "Inspected
By Sadie Bosheers," in a little teak box
on my desk, along with a Canadian coin
and one of my dog's puppy teeth.

I save it as oracle, this slip of paper
no bigger than my favorite
cookie fortune: "You are doomed
to be happy in wedlock." It's true
I'm doomed, Sadie, and I like to think
you might still find me happy enough,
though my elbows have begun to poke
through sleeves you certified so long ago.

Your signature is printed, not handwritten,
which to me just increases
your impartial grace. You had no need
to boast or qualify, just put down
one firm line to say that Sadie Bosheers
was here, on the job, living the life.
It's no statement about the honor
of hard toil, no suave calling card,
no complaint I read in your message.

Still, I accept the odd opaque blessing
of Sadie Bosheers—you step out calmly,
robed only in your own name, and meet

my dumb gaze. I pronounce that name,
and feel our separate dooms merge
in common air, both duly inspected,
both found somehow acceptable on this earth.

# The Dogs in Dutch Paintings

How shall I not love them, snoozing
right through the Annunciation? They inhabit
the outskirts of every importance, sprawl
dead center in each oblivious household.

They're digging at fleas or snapping at scraps,
dozing with noble abandon while a boy
bells their tails. Often they present their rumps
in the foreground of some martyrdom.

What Christ could lean so unconcernedly
against a table leg, the feast above continuing?
Could the Virgin in her joy match this grace
as a hound sagely ponders an upturned turtle?

No scholar at his huge book will capture
my eye so well as the skinny haunches,
the frazzled tails and serene optimism
of the least of these mutts, curled

in the corners of the world's dazzlement.

# The Poet Grows Less and Less Postmodern as Summer Advances

Winter's the time to topple icons,
see the stark asymmetry of it all
without leafy distraction. To disdain
romantic sap in its sullen retreat,
and question the self in its million
identical snowflakes.

But this afternoon, the maples giddy
with new leafage, ladybugs
traversing my shoe as I hike
under restive clouds, I feel
like a single bee commanding a rose,
so self-involved and magnetic,

I nearly feel I should dance a dance
to tell of pollen unimaginable.

I feel fit for the weedy slopes still above me.

My iambic heart almost skips a beat
at the calypso of today's dandelion spread,
and I hardly mind the oak's not loving me,

or the fox with her kits scattering
into the woods at my foot fall.

I'm the product of vast historical forces,
poor me, windstorms greater
than any encyclopedia. I say bravo
to that, and a little wow like a mosquito.

I accept my destiny exactly as milkweed
approves of the mud.

And there's nothing tardy,
nothing new about that.

# JEFFREY SKINNER

## 1997

Jeffrey Skinner engages the reality of other people in such a way that his poems are genuine disclosures of what is often hidden to our eyes: that we not only can, but that we must, hear the beating of hearts other than our own. The Eastern Orthodox Christian saint of the seventh century, Isaac of Syria, says: "The seeking for our own esteem is the cause of all our grief." And so Skinner's poems are peopled; that is, his poems escape the solipsism of the modern lyric by giving all its art to the reality of other people. Hence, his poems have the ontological strength to bear all our weight because they bring us all the weight of personhood genuinely and beautifully attended-to.

—Donald Sheehan

# The New Music Concert: A Drinking Dream

The composer began to speak about the aspens
which had inspired his upcoming piece,
but stopped suddenly in the middle of a word
and confessed that he did not know an aspen
from an oak, had never laid eyes,
could not pick one out of a mugbook of trees
if his life depended, etcetera—he really
gave an eloquent apologia, before breaking
completely into sobs, his tux shirt
bending in little waves. The audience
was stunned—excruciating discomfort!—
and did not know where to turn. A man
with shaved head whipped out a cellphone
and whispered calm instructions to an underling.
The opposing hands of newlyweds
drifted toward each others' inner thighs.
The woman who had commissioned
the new music sat grandly motionless,
a Victorian mansion, gutted by fire. Stagehands
did what they could, moving the spotlight
around the floor, but the composer
would wander back into the light, weeping
and looking down at his hands in disgust,
as if he had dipped them in egg batter. Finally
a member of the brass section, a beauty
who had once been the composer's lover,
leapt up and dragged the composer
into the wings. The curtain of burgundy velvet
descended like a soft guillotine, cutting
off the whole sad affair. Then some
pale guy tiptoed out and announced

that after a short intermission the program
would resume. But I'd had enough. I walked
across the avenue to a bar, the dark kind
with knife scars on the mahogany railing,
and ordered a double. "Double what?," asked
the bartender. "Double Aspen," I said, not knowing
what I was saying. But it turns out there is
such a drink, which, the bartender whispered,
if it doesn't kill you will make you famous.

# My Son the Cicada

Wonder if the birds exchanging verses
from trees on opposite corners of the garden
even hear my son the cicada
sawing terribly his tree in the middle.
Only if his sound means food or love to them,
or warning, I'd bet. Today the sky is clear
as mercy in retrospect, maybe that's
what all the singing's about. Still, I feel
badly that I can do nothing, nothing for one
of my own. And now my son the cicada
has halted construction. Wonder if he's
packed his little toolbox and gone
home to the wife and kids, complaining
about the indifference of co-workers,
how his best efforts go unnoticed, in deference
to the mockingbird and other flashy stars
of flight. Wonder if he'll go out
drinking at the abandoned picnic table
tonight, side by side in the liqueur
of spilled Coke, with his pal the horsefly.
Wonder if when he finally makes it
to human incarnation he'll ever sit on this
second floor porch, looking out at hills with folded
shadows, comparing them to brains.
Wonder if he'll inherit my human sickness,
abstraction. Wonder if he'll remember me.

# Carver

There was no landscape so hard
he could not return
with its poetry.

And there it was—the champagne
hidden in the bathroom,
the blocked ear, the peacock

strutting through
the laborer's dining room;
everything we had missed

out of self-regard
or loftiness. People who die
in the stories die simply,

for no point, and those left
can only comfort
not turn away. Now the teacher

leaves the room, and the students
hush under the loud clock.
Whatever they can see

through the window,
the flat earth too poor and dry
for growing, they are on their own.

# The Invalid

One of the old songs playing tag
kept inside by persistent rain
which, a billion drops striking a billion leaves
so close on each other's watery heels

sounds as one continuous
tattering rush, a waterfall surround
*and I wish, and I wish, and I wish*
says the slick grass darkening, or at least

that's what the man in his skin hears
whose nurse dozes like a white fly,
who coughs, hums, continues: always, still
trying to speak for the elements.

# Something Smaller

All along I have believed in the everlasting.
Oh yes. But if you ask me the everlasting *what?*
I come immediately to the end of language.
In Delaware we lived on the coast, where the shore
still aligns its foamy buffer
with the ocean's theory of everything.
Where the lighthouse I'd walk to with visiting friends
keeps up its stubborn *yes no, yes no.*
And the sea, where dream may begin as water
then turn to salt-stiff hair, flavors inward
though it's been twelve years.

Oh yes. But I don't believe the sea is what I mean
by everlasting. Nor do I mean lighthouse, dream,
friend, shore. Something smaller—the day Sarah, Bonnie,
Laura and I returned from the beach
and in the cold spray of the backyard shower
the girls shrieked, and when they shook their blond heads
*No*, I remember the flung drops, flashing in the sun.

# Closed Head Wounds

The boxer retires, buys himself a house
in the mountains, red with black shutters. He still gets up
to jog the dirt road early, though not so early
as before, not so fast. Flowers among the weeds
banking the road on either side may be the flowers
*of* weeds, he doesn't know. Tiny yellow, white,
orange, and one so harshly violet it hurts the eye,
his favorite. He must buy a book of names.
Townspeople are curt without malice, they answer
questions, they make change while turning
back to local friends. Why? Maybe it comes
from living in mountains, he thinks, every horizon
like a muscled back, and who could strut or brag
like homeboys when each morning you drive to work
through *that*? Because some woman told him to,
he has hung suet outside his bedroom window.
When he wakes sometimes half-dreaming
a hummingbird whisks in, like a left hook, stops
short and drinks. He watches, propped on an elbow.
Birds remind him of fast hands, back when he
was no opponent, but took the number-two guy
twelve rounds and almost won. Should have. *Did,* many
said—and not just handlers. The air here like water,
the water like air, cold gusts off the mountains
you inhale against thirst. It's perfect for training,
he catches himself thinking. But that's gone. Ah,
too much has been knocked from his head:
the way feet move against a left-hander, words,
music, sons, women, years. He towels off,
inspects his face in the bathroom mirror, the old
kind: wooden box with mirrored door, screwed to the wall.

Clown ears, wide nose, scars like troughs dug deep
into each brow. *So this is the life*, he thinks, *the rest
of it* . . . And the creature in the box grins back.

# The Moving Sidewalk Is Ending

Why do people stand in the center and not move
when you, toting shoulder bag and briefcase (laptop)
are in a hurry, and a warm electronic female
voice has told them repeatedly to *stand to the right*
so that others might pass? —Like you, who face
the spring conference at which you'll present
a year's worth of office sweat and blood distilled
to one idea, complete with cybergraph and projections
of the future? Or you, whose phone rang like a loud zero
at 3 A.M., and sprint now to catch your father's soul,
a white flag (you imagine) slowly rippling above his white
body? Or you, lugging kids who've made you late
for your own true life before, putting the dirty flowers
of their hands in front of your eyes, whining again,
with that once-in-a-lifetime job in Nevada
six minutes from takeoff? Who are these people
in our way? It might have been better to take
the carpeted walk on either side—there you can thread
through the laggards at your own clipped pace,
you can outrun the grooved metal churning
which brings you only part way there in any case.
Then it ends. And you have to get off
and contend with them again, these human rocks
standing in the middle of the terminal hallway
as if it were a mountain pass, and you like water
must find a way around. Who are these idiots? Is there
any getting through to them? Don't they know your time
is limited, that if you could kill them without
consequence, to speed your departure, you would?

# The Inadequacy

A student from the upper West Side
wrote: "While I was doing the paper work
for the rental car I realized
I'd left my purse on the front seat.
I went back down to the garage, opened the car
and got it. An employee—this beefy lunk
rushed up, all hyper and officious.
'Fuck off,' I said, and he murmured *bitch*.
'What did you say?,' I said, and
*Bitch*, he said again, louder. I slapped him.
He slapped me, I slapped him back.
Then he beat me unconscious.
My nose will need surgery, but I'm
all right. Thanks for your words on my poems—
I do so need encouragement." I folded
the woman's letter and opened
my notebook. I was in the mountains
trying to work, which is what the established
call writing poems. A type of bee
I'd never seen clambered tiers of goldenrod;
I wrote that down. Clouds with silvered
hulls, angelic tugs, towed shadows
across the mountains. Another line.
The nervy dither of a moth through day lilies,
and so on . . . Who was this woman, that she broke
my morning into fragments—dumb, insentient
bits any idiot could see? If I'd been there,
I would've cold-cocked the guy,
Denise. Or maybe just run for help.
I hope at least I would've knelt to the cold
cement to stop your bleeding. But

who knows? The mountains have disappeared.
Poetry is such a human gun.

# SUE ELLEN THOMPSON

## 1998

I n her work, Sue Ellen Thompson explores those hidden
yet determinative connections among artistic, domestic,
and social relations: connections where every intensity is
comprehended, and every comprehension is made intense
and new. In a recent essay she spoke movingly of the friend-
ship between Robert Frost and Edward Thomas, a friendship
made eloquent to us by her comprehension of an intensity
between these two poets that was always seeking to under-
stand itself more fully. In her poems, she gives us this
comprehended depth of intensity in all the world in the
form of a bright, delicate clarity—to use the final lines of a
Bill Wenthe poem: "she holds / a new, delicate, two-note
breathing."

—Donald Sheehan

# Living at the Frost Place

The day my daughter leaves for California,
I'm three hundred miles north
in the Franconia, New Hampshire farmhouse
where Robert Frost lived with his wife
and four young children. I don't call
to tell her to pack vitamins and sunblock,
I don't ask what airline or what flight she's on.
She's old enough to make her way
from one end of the continent to another.

I spend the morning writing
at my makeshift summer desk on the verandah,
Mount Lafayette a hazy blue reminder
of the obstacles that pierce the sky at intervals
from here to the Sierras. The Morris chair
Frost sat in when he wrote the great poems
of his middle years stands brooding
in the parlor, flanked by manuscripts
and letters in glass cases—stern reminders
that I've reached the point in life where work
must come before the fretful agitations of a parent.

I take the silkscreened print she made me
for my birthday—an abstract latticework
in red and black like synapses, or the mysteries
of blood—down from the mantel and replace it
with a photo of the poet on the peak of Lafayette
surrounded by his children: disapproving
Lesley; Marjorie, who died of complications
following childbirth; Carol, melancholy boy
who shot himself; Irma, terrified
of men, who went insane.

# Echo Rock Farm

The redwood table with its beach umbrella, bleached to beige,
is breaking down, its crossed legs wobbly with age.

My mother reads beneath it in her loosened suit of flesh.
My father, from the sound of things, is cutting grass.

The eighteenth century cape they bought in their late fifties,
as if they knew they'd have these twenty years of living

exactly as they please, sags perceptibly earthward
just beyond the pool, blue mosaic sloping toward

the deep end's deeper shade. The mower lapses
into silence as I shift position on my raft.

From inside, a shout: my father's *Hoo!*
as he wipes his face with a folded hankie—or is it *Sue!*

as his heart makes a fist? I lock eyes
with my mother. The fitted sheet of haze across the sky

quivers, as if suddenly snapped taut. A few strokes
and I've pulled my body from the element that holds

it, sprinting across the bristling, just-cut grass,
traversing the screened-in porch, where sunlight lies in slats

on wicker rockers, dozing cats. Then, in as calm
a voice as I can muster: *Daddy? Pop?*

The kitchen cool and gleaming cleanly, whitely, bluely:
Nothing. Bedroom with its made bed. Surely

He would have called out a second time. Or maybe not.
Forbidden fragrance of the bathroom from my childhood—*Pop?*

—a mix of cigarettes and urine while he shaved.
One room opening into another's silence, order, shade.

The singing of a whetstone: my father in his shop,
bent over the mower blade. *Is that you, Pop?*

A few hours later: packing, heading north.
My mother brings me leftovers: cold pork,

mashed potatoes, foreshortened baseball bat
of a zucchini, nectarines she claims they'll never eat.

My father's busy loading my truck
with firewood—sour, muscular oak

so dry you see its tendons. *You'll get
some chilly nights up there in August.* The windshield's wet

from where he's washed it. Then he disappears inside
while my mother watches me roll backward down the drive.

Low sun swipes its topaz brush over the scene,
repeated endlessly each time a child leaves,

at the same time performing an even more miraculous feat,
transforming—in seconds instead of years—her hair from Jackie

Kennedy sable to the roan of her sixties to an ashy
gold that has more of the time of year in it than gray.

# After the Accident

The old rose-colored Buick turns in
past the rows of slush-covered cars
with webbed windshields and wrinkled doors.
My father steps out, unfolding himself
on the ice-slick asphalt with an old bird's grace
and stands, hands at the back of his waist,
leaning against the sky. My mother,
buoyed along by her puffed blue coat,
is all scurry and search as she hurries
toward me through the glass door marked
"Service," her arms already rising
from her sides. Swept up into

the car's small warmth, I let myself
be taken to lunch, I let them order for me—
a cheeseburger in the golden arms
of mounded onion rings, a cookie the size
of my own spread palm
weighted with chocolate. I eat
and I eat, as if I'd been trapped
in that snow-choked ravine for days,
as if food were love and I could absorb it,
turning it into flesh the way
they turned their love into me.
But seeing all that is left—a thinnish woman
in her forties without a car, without
even a purse, they must think
it is not enough. So they feed me and I
eat, and all that keeps me from an infant's sleep
is who will carry me home when they are gone?

# Fin de Siècle

A man I've loved for years
arrives to take me out for dinner, beard

a mitten on my etched and powdered cheek.
The talk right off is all of books

and children. Then, over a brisk sorbet
and decaf, he grows shifty-eyed, the way

a child does, tells me that he's tired tonight—
this the man who telephoned at midnight,

skated the length of the interstate and made it to my bed
by dawn on more than one occasion—says,

a little sheepishly, he's thinking he might drop
me off and head for home. I intend to stop

him by whatever means I've not already been denied.
But like the bellied August sky

that keeps its grief and fury pending
over the low hills for days without sending

a bolt earthward, or drenching anyone below,
I don't. I let him let me go.

# Parted

End of a long journey—Perth, Tasmania, Sydney,
Auckland, L.A.—our bodies folded and pressed
up together like books, Volumes One and
Two, all the way to New York. I followed my husband down
the long ramp, suddenly chilled by damp,
east coast air, along the conveyor
to Baggage Claim. *You stay here while I*
*call the shuttle*, he said, but I followed him
anyway, drawing the carry-ons close to my ankles
next to the phone booth, giving the weight of my shoulder
to where his oxford-cloth shirt warmed the glass.

*Save me a seat*, he said when the blue van arrived,
so I spread out my cardigan, arms flung wide,
while he herded our bags to the rear.
A foreign couple, older than we, the woman clutching
her husband's thick arm, tried to climb
in beside me. I said in my most polite English
that I was sorry, this seat was saved for my husband.
The wife looked so frightened—as if I had said,
*Men to the left, women and children*
*go right*, as if I had swept him out
of her sight with the butt of my rifle. The man

took the only seat left, up front. His wife
sat three rows behind, her eyes quick as birds
if he tilted his head or cast his shy glance
at the driver. I pressed my temporal bone into
my husband's sharp clavicle—as I had done
coming back on the ferry from Rottnest Island, swells
of the Indian Ocean so huge I feared

the ship might break at the seam
between my brow and his shoulder. We had come
this far together: I would not be parted
from him for such a small thing as shame.

# The Mother's Dream

Rushed all morning, I leave the house
without buttoning my coat, drive into town,
am waiting at a stoplight when I see
the shadow-mother in the car behind me
twist and lean to check her sleeping infant.
Suddenly I know—more fundamentally
than I've known anything—I've left
my baby home. The dream proceeds,
an underwater dance in which each step
is languid, hampered, infuriatingly
slow. Traffic swirls like storm debris,
my car is blunt and useless as a raft.

Awakened by the shriek
of the morning's first shower—
angry mix of air and water
in the bathroom pipes—I hear
the sullen movements of my full-limbed,
full-grown daughter in her senior year.
She's overslept, she's overtired,
I know that if I try to speak to her
I'll get an angry, muffled *Mom*—her signal
for an end to conversation. So I let
myself fall backward into sleep,
and like a book whose pages separate
just where the bookmark's wedged
its narrow foot, the dream takes up
the story of my mothering, along with its
familiar consequence: I never get her back.

# The Empty Room

Unable to sleep, my husband gropes
for his reading glasses and book.
He tiptoes into our daughter's room—
the bed freshly made in the wake
of her leaving for college, the windows
stripped of their curtains for washing—
and draws back the dinosaur sheets,
slipping into the crescent shape
of her absence.

              I think of him there:
middle-aged, the gray with its fingers
laced deep in his beard, little half-glasses
crouched low on the ridge of his nose.
Just before dawn, I go to him,
lowering my body into his
backwards, pressing my shoulder blades
into his chest, my hips
into the hollow of his, the curve
of my calves against his hard shins,
lashing my body to his as I did
in the tumult of our twenties, when all
we longed for was an end to the storm,
when all we knew of loss was to turn
in the night and find the other one gone.

# The Leaving

I lie on the bathroom floor, my bed
two damp towels and weep
for my daughter, her first trip away
from me over dark water,
the suitcase with its soft limbs
of denim and corduroy adrift
in the plane's loose belly. I weep
for the islands she'll cross in her sleep,
for the fishing boats scattered like rice-grains.
I weep for the city of London, its domes
and spires obscured now by slabs of glass,
no longer the city of my marriage,
my daughter already a curled fist of fern in my belly
as I climbed the steps to the registry,
where Queen Victoria brooded
in dun-colored marble. From the kitchen window
of my flat in Greenwich I could see
the tangled chain of students from the local school
for the retarded meander down the street
behind their teacher and I vowed,
*Just send me one who's perfect and I'll never*
*show her any less than love.*
                                Yesterday
she flung an angry arm at me as I was showing her
the proper way to roll and pack her clothing.
*All you care about is order,* she accused me,
the vast and cluttered canvas of her room
its own rebuke. Then she slammed
her bedroom door so hard
bits of caulk sprung
from the molding. When she left today,

I was out pulling weeds, my thumbnail pushed deep
in the earth's soft flesh, my face sprayed with dirt,
the strength of my back locked against
each root-hair's fierce foothold. She stood
in the drive, her luggage like huge stones
on either side. Now she's off to where
my life with her began and I weep
for what she'll find there, the wanting and the
getting, the having and the turning it away.

# MARY RUEFLE

## 1999

In her poems, Mary Ruefle writes a lyric made at once graceful and frightening by its fierce commitment to what Charles Williams, in his remarkable Arthurian poems, terms that "path of linear necessity" called *speed*. A Ruefle poem moves at such a speed that "the necessity of being" is communicated fully in the necessity of acceleration. But so graceful and so poised are her poems that they seem to have all the time in the world. And so they embody this wonderful paradox wherein grace and speed are kindred sisters—and her paradoxical art reveals the surprise of all paradox: *para* (parallel) *doxa* (glory).

—Donald Sheehan

# 10 April

The young cherry tree is naked and alone
trying to hide from the cold night.
Which is impossible so the man has come
and put his arms around the tree.
He is wearing the clothes of his dead mother,
a white slip, a thin buff-colored kimono,
a heavier black one on top.
He begins to tremble with all the anxiety
a young tree feels in the spring,
his face white with rice powder,
the wind blowing hair across it
without breaking a strand.
He isn't a man pretending to be a tree,
he's a man honoring a woman
who is trying to become a tree.
Only once does he open his mouth:
there is rouge on his tongue
as if he's been eating cherries off the ground
and is deeply ashamed, but purified
like a well.

# My Beautiful Spider Bite

You kissed me in front of the whole regime
arduous, disconnected
on the inside of my leg
in just a matter of seconds
every bit of inattention
right down to the smallest particle of airborne thought
was swept away  My beautiful spider bite
digital itch, inexpressible urge
wound I long to wound
you broke a crystal bottle of brew on my head
I walked through a curtain of beads
together we studied the menu, first fine print then big
it has been a year since we met
we will not go to the doctor's today
but, my brown recluse
come home, come home
one grows stupid with sorrow
that's insupportable

# No Comparison

In the dream your face was rippling everywhere
like banners of Mao.
How unlucky you are not to be loved
by a million people, but only by one,
one who likes the word Mao
out of a million words.
The cat knows.
The sun sometimes
finds its way through a river of garbage
spilling down an alley
and lights on a litter.
And anyone who chances by stops to marvel.
The hairs of your head are all numbered.
You are of more value than many sparrows.
Mao thought we could make a difference.
Many of his countrymen thoughtfully concluded
that would be true—if we existed.
So he rippled there for awhile.
Those that ate manna are dead.
So it is not your face I remember
but the wind—
it lifted the hairs of your head
and I was able to count them
it dispersed the sparrows in the square
and sent them in different directions
it ran through the banners
like a hand on the back of a cat
and it woke me suddenly
like a vivid face.
May it live ten thousand years.

# Furthurness

An oak coffin covered with vines
carried on moss in a farm cart

A dusty coffin in a yellow wagon
with bright red wheels going down
the painted road

A glass coffin stifled by roses

Raining, and in the film version
an unknown god stood at a distance
watching, got in his car and left

The little black urn before
a spray of orchids in the alcove

They laid a bunch of violets at her throat
closed the white coffin
carried it out the rear door
through buttercups down to the grave

The musicians are drunk and play
loudly, stumbling down the street

Six men with sore arms

The family in a rowboat:
the coffin inhabiting the mind

Or ashes streaming like a scarf from the convertible

Or, the chorus breaks out in excelsis

Or, the soloist sang like a dilated eye

Stunning din of a sob

Salt pork on a wound

Is it ordure to speak of the widow's grief?

Who drags herself back
through a field so thick with vetch
it gives a purple tint over two or three acres
You could run through them for hours
but one thing is certain from her face
she does not want you to

Furthermore, there are pies on the table waiting

# The Shorthand of Sensation

By a window, through which is seen
a landscape, an old man with a deformed
nose, dressed in a red robe trimmed with
fur, his head towards the right, looks down
with infinite longing and bitter irony
at his pudding, who in profile to the left,
with curly cusps of cream escaping from under
a red cherry, reaches up to kiss the thought.

# Among the Musk Ox People

There were aesthetes, which means
I was forced to eat a hard peach,
commissioned to paint a twelve foot abstraction
based on watching host cells collaborate
in bacterial infection, and at night
chewed the soles of their mukluks
till they were soft again.
If I ventured outside the igloo
and saw a celebrity
I felt so inferior
I wanted to die.
To conceal my envy
I was given dark glasses.
If, on the other hand, I encountered
someone to whom I was vastly superior,
one of those ill-clad, raving, wandering hags,
I felt ashamed and wanted to die.
To appease my guilt
they were given by the Elders a little of my grub.
If I met with an Ordinary,
someone not dissimilar to myself,
with dissatisfactions roughly the same,
I felt the world was senseless
supporting so many look alikes
and again I asked to die:
life reached a maddening peak
out there on the ice when
we were hunting and could move only our eyes.
Still, like a seal reaching his blowhole
in the dark, every seventy-two hours
I came to my senses for thirteen minutes

and continued to live with the knowledge
that deep in the oyster bed of my blood
layered spheres continued to build round
my name, cold, calciferous, and forgotten.
When the Giant Orphan At the Bottom Of The Sea
appeared in my dreams,
demanding I write the story
of three generations of Ox women
resulting in the birth of a performance artist,
I knew I would need a knife, gun, needles,
kettle, scissors and soap,
and gave up, at last, my finest skins.
I made my escape across the shrouded inlet
away from those who believe that outside
our thoughts there is only mist,
and with my skills at flensing,
never feared for the future.

# The Tragic Drama of Joy

Late that night it rained so hard the world
     seemed flattened for good.
But the grocer knew the earth had a big gut
     and could hold more than enough.
When he went out to receive a shipment of cat food
     the stays of his umbrella were bent.
It took some time to fix them and when he got to his shop
     the truck had already left.
On a whim he went inside and brought home
     a bottle of wine for his wife.
Have you gone crazy? she said. They didn't uncork it,
     but he felt something nonetheless.
That wonderful *click* his umbrella had made
     when it finally opened for good!

# Silk Land

Nothing's happened, there are no examples.
At most I feel an exceptionally light bug
has been bothering me.
It's dead on the maternity ward
and I've never even *seen* bougainvillea
so this gardening rag is a bust.
There's a rustle of forms.
Aline comes in at midnight
and gives me a penny for my thoughts.
She's like a mid-Atlantic Coke machine
that's out of order. Bob comes in at six
and tells me about the weekend.
He screwed behind sandbags, lurched
down the beach, blacked out
but didn't drown.
I crawl straight back to the depths of
my mother's drawer, sunk among the lingerie.

# MARK COX

## 2000

In his poems, Mark Cox achieves an impossible conjunction: he brings a shrewd self-confidence into the realm of deepest vulnerability. Consequently, the shrewdness becomes lyrically open, while the vulnerability becomes highly intelligent. Horace, that greatest of Latin lyric poets—the poet that Robert Frost prized, all his life, above every other poet—placed lyric form even above epic and tragedy: because, said Horace, lyric form recalls the origins of all our courage. The shrewd lyricism of Mark Cox partakes of this courage.

— Donald Sheehan

# Things My Grandfather Must Have Said

I want to die in the wintertime,
make the ground regret it,
make the backhoe sweat.

January. Blue Monday
after the holiday weekend.
I want it to be hard on everybody.

I want everyone to have a headache
and the traffic to be impossible.
Back it up for miles, Jesus.

I want steam under the hood, bad directions,
cousins lost, babies crying, and sleet.
I want a wind so heavy their umbrellas howl.

And give me some birds, pigeons even,
anything circling for at least half an hour,
and plastic tulips and a preacher who stutters

"Uh" before every word of Psalm 22.
I want to remind them just how bad things are.
Spell my name wrong on the stone, import

earthworms fat as Aunt Katie's arms
and put them under the folding chairs.
And I want a glass coffin,

I want to be wearing the State of Missouri
string tie that no one else liked.... God,
I hope the straps break

and I fall in with a thud. I hope
the shovel slips out of my son's hands.
I want them to remember I don't feel anything.

I want the food served straight from my garden.
I want the head of the table set. I want
everyone to get a pennant that says,

"Gramps was the greatest,"
and a complete record of my mortgage payments
in every thank-you note.

And I want to keep receiving mail for 13 years,
all the bills addressed to me,
old friends calling every other month

to wonder how I am.
Then I want an earthquake or rising water table,
the painful exhumation of my remains.

I want to do it all again.

I want to die the day before something truly
important happens and have my grandson say:
What would he have thought of that.

I want you all to know how much I loved you.

# Sonata

At ninety, the piano plays him.
He's like a man by the sea
the wind knows it must wear down,
sculpt to a profile,
then fill out again,
billowing his sleeves and trouser legs
into a younger musculature.
Over and again, the music reddens
then greys, the part
in its hair shifting left to center
until those few blades of sea grass
are all that's left to be
combed over the rocks,
and the thin fingers skitter,
leaving impressions in the keyboard
that waves wash level,
cleansing its audience of shell halves,
now glistening, now scoured dry.
And the house, the house just outside
this sonata's frame,
begs him to turn around
to pick his way back
along the stony runner,
his hands stopping his ears.
But, at ninety, the music plays the piano,
which plays the man, who finally, fearlessly,
plays himself, which is the landscape,
which is everything that ends.

# Grain

*(after Vallejo and Justice)*

I may die in Kansas on a cloudless day—
one of those wholesome weekends
between wheat conventions and gun shows
glazed over with plenty.
I may simply buckle
beneath the gold-flecked eyes of a carhop,
grasp the little window tray
and never rise again.
The living blue of the sky
will no longer glance off my body,
my lips assume the tinge of Welch's grape juice,
my food grow cold.
These will bear witness to me:
twenty distracted tee-ball players
in three different makes of minivan.
Mark Cox will be dying. I will want
to utter "ambulance" as a last word on earth,
but it will sound like "ambitious."
I will want to say "my heart"
but it will sound like "my art."
I will not want to leave you, love.
Our son, even if grown,
will be inching up the stair rail—
shin-deep in my workboots,
he will be going up
while I am going down
and like a snapping turtle in a $2.00 butterfly net,
I will refuse the new world.
I will not want to leave my shirts emptied
over the backs of chairs,

I will not want to leave my toothbrush
leaning dry against yours—
I will have to be taken from you, love,
carried off by strong men
whose fathers sowed the grain fields around me,
it will take three of them, love,
I will remain so heavy with need for you,
so stubbornly loyal—
and even though I will be no more
than a quickly scrawled number next to the phone,
no more than a last breath not fully exhaled
I will root myself in this earth of ours.
I will not rise through the air
nor dissolve into ground water,
I will not yearn for release
nor turn my face to the sky.
I will have to be taken on my side, love,
the way we lay together
when I was alive.

# Black Olives

Cooking was, at first, a problem not worth solving;
he wasn't really hungry and it took days.
to eat the leftovers. But after the funeral,
while opening a can of soup, he understood
that despite fifty years of meals,
there was not one morsel left.

There are no doubt some several million persons
to whom this did not matter much
in October of 1977.
But in the grayed light of her kitchen,
at the faux marble-topped table for two,
my grandfather added and multiplied and estimated,
and when he was done, proposed
to have an accurate accounting
of how many tons grandmother had cooked.
It was something he had to know.
And he could not be bothered to eat until he did.

And even this was not enough, no, he had to illustrate,
he had to concretize, he had to guess how many silos
her labor would have filled. How many acres
were planted, how many loaves were baked, how many
animals, by type, had marched two by two into our mouths.

When he finished it was dusk and his soup was cold.
He let us have a pizza delivered—mushroom and black olives—
and we laughed, a little weakly, at just how much grandma
would have hated what he'd done—

how she always glazed over when he computed mileage per gallon.
But she had loved black olives—those tiny bitter, hollowed hearts—
she'd eaten how many, let's see, how many would that be...?

# Poem at 40

Windwashed—as if standing next to the highway,
a truck long as the century sweeping by,
all things at last bent in the same direction.
An opening, as if all
the clothes my ancestors ever wore
dry on lines in my body:
wind-whipped, parallel with the ground,
some sleeves sharing a single clothespin
so that they seem to clasp hands,
seem to hold on.

And now that I can see
up the old women's dresses,
there's nothing but a filtered light.
And now that their men's smoky breath
has traversed the earth,
it has nothing to do with them.
And now that awkward, fat tears of rain
slap the window screen,
now that I'm naked too,
cupping my genitals, tracing with a pencil
the blue vein between my collar bone and breast,
I'll go to sleep when I'm told.

# Pulsar

There is an unsettling dailiness
to letters of the dead—
they shook the rain from their umbrellas,
they dried their socks on radiators—
but like a gnat balanced
on the hair of their arms,
the pressure of death was always there,

and he who is left to read
now bears it also,
a constant usually assimilated
like the hum of the fluorescent light
he reads by,
becomes, now, irrevocable silence,
a door opening
onto the particular frictions of things:
wind streaming between eave vents,
rain thipping at glass,
his own blood just beneath the skin.

He, left living, opens his eyes
on another day he can't keep from happening,
every window an open wound
smeared with sunlight
the yellow of grass beneath a patio block,
birds bickering in the pom-poms
of trees that top his building,
and beyond, embedded light-years
in the unfathomed reaches of the psyche,
the cold, dead planets of his wife and children,
the meteorites of friends and family,

all the broken techno-junk and orbiting debris,
circle their dying star—
he, who cannot move to lift his brush to his teeth,
yet who shudders with the energy he has no choice
but to have.

The Salvation Army has been by
for its pink garbage bags of clothing—
in thrift shops, city-wide,
the belt buckles, the bracelets, the Tonka trucks
and reading glasses—all the shaped minerals and metals,
the leathers, the woods, have been racked and tagged,
are being dispersed
to live out their time, like light in space,
as mere projections of their origins,
their courses fixed, though severed utterly,
their presence felt, though undetected,
irreducible and gone.

# The Will

*I am about to—or, I am going to—die:*
*either expression is correct.*
　　　　　　　—Dominique Bouhours
　　　　　　　(French grammarian, d. 1702)

Tilting my head, watching car lights wind
down the mountain, I realize
how easily the mountain moves.
It's in flames on the glass of our window,
like our faces in those flames,
while the one cloud, black-lit, and pausing
briefly along the top of the mountain,
rains out there beyond us,
yet inside us too.

What we have is here to be seen through.
Cinnamon tea welling in our spoons,
steam rising
off the dog still trembling near the hearth—
we've made plans.

I sought for a town among mountains, once;
a little Greek town where the wind
would put its soft mouth to the houses
in the one chord I could sleep to.
When the windows chattered restless in casings there,
it would feel good to shiver in the dark with them.
And upon closing my eyes I would see through the earth
and fall to a space where time ruled so gently
that the stars could cease their blinking. A car
turning the corner could lay its white hand on my forehead,
but I'd know it was God.

"'Light! More light!'" you ask,
"Whose last words were those?"
Then, "'Put out that bloody cigarette...'"
which were H. H. Munro's. How easily
that German bullet translated his individuated voice,
even as he attempted to stay entrenched in the dark.

Today, when the dog dropped your stick
at my feet, and shook the lake from himself
I was shocked by the cold he'd just as soon return to.
But when I looked at the water it was a Greek woman

standing and smoothing her dress, and I knew
that wherever we're going it won't be cold at all,
it won't be permanent. The wavering, the flickering,
the motion is what matters.

# ADVISORY BOARD

CavanKerry Press is grateful to the following individuals, whose invaluable contributions to *The Breath of Parted Lips*, Volume I, made its publication possible.

# CONTRIBUTORS

JULIE AGOOS is the author of *Above the Land* (Yale University Press, 1987), selected by James Merrill for the Yale Series of Younger Poets Award and winner of the 1987 Towson State University Award for Literature; and of *Calendar Year* (Sheep Meadow Press, 1996). A graduate of Harvard University and the Writing Seminars at the Johns Hopkins University, she has taught Creative Writing and English at Johns Hopkins University and Princeton University and is currently Associate Professor of English at Brooklyn College/CUNY. A native of Cambridge, Massachusetts, she lives in Princeton, New Jersey.

SHARON BRYAN has published three books of poems: *Salt Air* (Wesleyan, 1983), *Objects of Affection* (Wesleyan, 1987), and *Flying Blind* (Sarabande, 1996). She is also the editor of *Where We Stand: Women Poets on Literary Tradition* (Norton, 1995). Her awards include two National Endowment for the Arts fellowships in poetry. She has taught at the University of Houston, the Warren Wilson M.F.A. Program for Writers, Dartmouth College, the University of Washington, Memphis State University, Western Michigan University, Kalamazoo College, Ohio University, the University of Missouri-St. Louis, and Wichita State University. She lives in Port Townsend, Washington.

ROBERT CORDING teaches English and Creative Writing at Holy Cross College, where he is Professor of English and poet-in-residence. He has published three collections of poems: *Life-list*, which won the Ohio State University Press/Journal Award, in 1987; *What Binds Us to This World* (Cooper Beech Press, 1991); and *Heavy Grace* (Alice James, 1996). He has received fellowships from the National Endowment for the Arts, the Connecticut Commission of the Arts, and Bread Loaf. His poems have appeared in *The Nation*, *Poetry*, *DoubleTake*, and *The New Yorker*. He lives in Woodstock, Connecticut, with his wife and three children.

MARK COX chairs the Department of Creative Writing at the University of North Carolina, Wilmington, and teaches in the Vermont College M.F.A. in Writing Program. His honors include a Whiting Writers' Award, a Pushcart

Prize, the Oklahoma Book Award, the Society of Midland Authors Poetry Prize, and a Burlington-Northern Faculty Achievement Award. He has served as poetry editor of *Passages North* and *Cimarron Review* and has received fellowships from the Kansas Arts Commission, the Vermont Council on the Arts, and the Bread Loaf Writers' Conference. Mr. Cox has published poems in many national anthologies and in such magazines as *Poetry, The American Poetry Review, The North American Review, The New England Review*, and *Harvard Review*. His books are *The Barbells of the Gods* (Ampersand, 1988), *Smoulder* (Godine, 1989), and *Thirty-Seven Years from the Stone* (Pitt Poetry Series, 1998). He lives in Wilmington, North Carolina.

Born in South Bend, Indiana, in 1931, JOHN ENGELS attended the University of Notre Dame and the Iowa Writers' Workshops, from which he graduated in 1957. He has been a member of the English faculty at St. Michael's College in Colchester, Vermont, since 1962, as well as having taught at Randolph-Macon Woman's College, Middlebury College, Emory University, and Hollins College where he was Writer in Residence in 1996. He has published ten volumes of poems, the most recent of which include *Walking to Cootehill* (Middlebury/University Press of New England, 1992), *Big Water* (Lyons & Burford, 1994), and *Sinking Creek* (Lyons Books, 1997). A new collection, *House and Garden*, will be published next year by the University of Notre Dame Press. Mr. Engels has received two National Endowment for the Arts grants, a Guggenheim Fellowship (1980), a Fulbright Fellowship (Yugoslavia, 1985), as well as a Rockefeller Foundation residency at Bellagio in 1991. *Weather-Fear: New and Selected Poems, 1958–1982* (University of Georgia Press) was a finalist for the Pulitzer Prize in 1983, while *Cardinals in the Ice Age* (Graywolf Press) was an American Poetry Series selection in 1987.

KATHY FAGAN, author of the National Poetry Series selection *The Raft* (Dutton, 1985), teaches in the MFA Program at The Ohio State University, where she also co-edits *The Journal*. Her most recent collection, *MOVING & ST RAGE*, won the Vassar Miller Prize and was published by University of North Texas Press in 1999. Her work has appeared in literary magazines such as *FIELD, The Kenyon Review, The Missouri Review, The New Republic, Ploughshares*, and *The Paris Review*, and in the anthology *Extraordinary Tide: New Poetry by American Women* (Columbia University Press, 2001). Fagan is the recipient of fellowships from the Ingram Merrill Foundation, the National Endowment for the Arts, and the Ohio Arts Council.

CHRISTOPHER GILBERT, unlike many poets, makes his living not as a teacher of literature or a teacher of poetry, but as a psychologist. For the past dozen years he has worked with children, adults, and families in a variety of therapeutic settings. His first book, *Across the Mutual Landscape*, was published in 1984 by Graywolf Press and received the Walt Whitman Award.

DAVID GRAHAM was born and raised in Johnstown, New York. His education took him to two places associated with Robert Frost: Dartmouth College, from which he graduated in 1975, and Amherst, Massachusetts, where he earned an M.F.A. at the University of Massachusetts in 1980. His poems have appeared in six collections: *Magic Shows* (Cleveland State, 1986), *Common Waters* (Flume, 1986), *Second Wind* (Texas Tech., 1990), *Doggedness* (Devil's Millhopper, 1991), *Stutter Monk* (Flume, 2000), and *Greatest Hits 1975–2000* (Pudding House, 2001). With Kate Sontag, he has edited an anthology of essays, *After Confession: The Poet as Autobiographer*, which will be published by Graywolf in 2001. Since 1987, he has taught English at Ripon College in Ripon, Wisconsin, where he lives with his wife, Lee Shippey.

MARK HALLIDAY teaches at Ohio University. His books of poems are *Little Star* (William Morrow, 1987), which was a National Poetry Series selection; *Tasker Street* (University of Massachusetts Press, 1992), which won the Juniper Prize; and *Selfwolf* (University of Chicago Press, 1999). His critical study of Wallace Stevens, *Stevens and the Interpersonal*, was published by Princeton University Press in 1991.

ROBERT HASS served as Poet Laureate of the United States from 1995 to 1997. He is the author of several books of poetry, including *Field Guide* (Yale, 1973), *Praise* (Ecco, 1979), *Human Wishes* (Ecco, 1989), and *Sun Under Wood* (Ecco, 1996). A book of his essays, *Twentieth Century Pleasures*, received the National Book Critics Circle Award for Criticism in 1984. He has co-translated many of the works of Nobel Prize-winning Polish poet, Czeslaw Milosz, and has edited *Selected Poems: 1954–1986* by Thomas Transtrΰmer; *The Essential Haiku: Versions of Bashō, Buson, and Issa* (Ecco, 1995); and *Poet's Choice: Poems for Everyday Life* (Ecco, 1998). His many honors include a MacArthur Fellowship and two National Book Critics Circle Awards. He is a professor of English at the University of California, Berkeley.

DENIS JOHNSON was born in 1949 in Munich, Germany, and raised in Tokyo, Manila, and Washington. He has received many awards for his work, including a Lannan Fellowship in Fiction and a Whiting Writer's Award. He has published several books of poems, including *The Man Among the Seals, Inner Weather, The Incognito Lounge*, and *The Veil*. His most recent collection, *The Throne of the Third Heaven of the Nations Millennium General Assembly: Poems, Collected and New* appeared in 1995 from HarperCollins. His books of fiction include *Angels, The Stars at Noon, The Name of the World* (HarperCollins, 2000), and *Jesus' Son*, which was recently adapted into a major motion picture.

CLEOPATRA MATHIS was born and raised in Ruston, Louisiana. Her work has appeared widely in anthologies, magazines, and journals, including *The New Yorker, The New Republic, Poetry, American Poetry Review, Tri-Quarterly, The Georgia Review, Southern Poetry Review*, and the forthcoming *Columbia Anthology of Contemporary American Women's Poetry*. Four collections of her poems have been published by Sheep Meadow Press, which will also bring out her fifth book, *What To Tip the Boatman?*, in Spring 2001. Prizes for her work include a National Endowment for the Arts award, the Peter Lavin Award for Younger Poets from the Academy of American Poets, the Pushcart Prize, and a poetry fellowship from the Fine Arts Work Center in Provincetown. Since 1982, she has been Professor of English and Creative Writing at Dartmouth College.

WILLIAM MATTHEWS was born in Cincinnati, Ohio, in 1942. During his lifetime he published eleven books of poetry, including *Time & Money* (1996), which won the National Book Critics Circle Award and was a finalist for the Lenore Marshall Poetry Prize; *Selected Poems and Translations 1969–1991* (1992); *Blues If You Want* (1989); *A Happy Childhood* (1984); *Rising and Falling* (1979); *Sticks and Stones* (1975); and *Ruining the New Road* (1970). A twelfth collection was published posthumously as *After All: Last Poems* (Houghton Mifflin, 1998). He received fellowships from the Guggenheim and Ingram Merrill foundations, the National Endowment for the Arts, and the Lila Wallace-Reader's Digest Fund. He taught at several schools, including Wells College, Cornell University, the University of Colorado, and the University of Washington. At the time of his death he was a professor of English and director of the creative writing program at New York's City College. Mr. Matthews died of a heart attack on November 12, 1997, the day after his fifty-fifth birthday.

GARY MIRANDA was born in Bremerton, Washington, and was raised in the Pacific Northwest. He has taught at various institutions, including three years as a Fulbright Lecturer at the University of Athens, Greece, and five years as writer-in-residence at Reed College in Portland, Oregon, his current home.

His published works include two collections of poetry with Princeton University Press and a translation of Rilke's *Duino Elegies*. Among the numerous awards he has won for his poetry are nine awards from the Poetry Society of America, and his poetry has appeared in many magazines, including *The Atlantic Monthly*, *The New Yorker*, and *Poetry*. He has a new collection of poems due out from Zoland Books in Spring 2001 and is currently working on his third screenplay.

STANLEY PLUMLY was born in Barnesville, Ohio, in 1939, and grew up in the lumber and farming regions of Virginia and Ohio. His work has been honored with the Delmore Schwartz Memorial Award and nominations for the National Book Critics Circle Award, the William Carlos Williams Award, and the Academy of American Poets' Lenore Marshall Poetry Prize. He has received a Guggenheim Foundation Fellowship, National Endowment for the Arts Awards, Pushcart Prizes, and an Ingram-Merrill Foundation Award. He has taught at many universities around the country, including the Universities of Iowa, Michigan, and Washington; Ohio University; Princeton University; Columbia University; the University of Houston; and New York University. He is currently a Distinguished University Professor and Professor of English at the University of Maryland.

KATHA POLLITT, the first poet-in-residence at The Frost Place, is the author of *Antarctic Traveller* (Knopf, 1982), which won the National Book Critics Circle Award in Poetry; and *Reasonable Creatures: Essays on Women and Feminism* (Knopf, 1994). She has won many awards for her poetry and prose, including grants from the National Endowment for the Arts, the Guggenheim Foundation, and the Whiting Foundation. She writes a column for *The Nation*, "Subject to Debate," and lives in New York City with her daughter, Sophie, and the writer Paul Mattick.

PATTIANN ROGERS has published nine books, including *The Dream of the Marsh Wren: Writing as Reciprocal Creation*, published by Milkweed Editions in their Credo Series in 1999. Milkweed will also publish *Song of the World Becoming: New and Collected Poems* in 2001. *A Covenant of Seasons*, a collaboration with the artist Joellyn Duesberry, was published by Hudson Hills Press in 1998. Ms. Rogers has received two National Endowment for the Arts grants, a Guggenheim Fellowship, a Lannan Fellowship, three prizes from *Poetry*, two prizes from *Prairie Schooner*, and five Pushcart Prizes. The mother of two grown sons, she lives with her husband, a retired geophysicist, in Colorado.

MARY RUEFLE is the author of five books of poems, the most recent of which is *Post Meridian* (Carnegie-Mellon, 2000). She is the recipient of a Whiting Writers' Award, an Award in Literature from the American Academy of Arts and Letters, and a National Endowment for the Arts fellowship. She lives in Massachusetts.

MARY JO SALTER is the author of four books of poems, all published by Alfred A. Knopf. The most recent, *A Kiss in Space*, appeared in 1999. A recipient of Guggenheim, Amy Lowell, and Ingram Merrill Fellowships, she has served as Poetry Editor of *The New Republic*, and co-edited the fourth edition of *The Norton Anthology of Poetry* (1996). She is Emily Dickinson Lecturer in the Humanities at Mount Holyoke College, and lives with her family in Amherst, Massachusetts.

SHEROD SANTOS has written four books of poetry, *Accidental Weather* (Doubleday, 1982), *The Southern Reaches* (Wesleyan, 1989), *The City of Women* (Norton, 1993), and *The Pilot Star Elegies* (Norton, 1999), which was both a National Book Award Finalist and one of five nominees for The New Yorker Book Award. His poems appear regularly in such journals as *The New Yorker, The Paris Review, The Nation, Poetry,* and *The Yale Review*. A collection of his essays, *A Poetry of Two Minds* (University of Georgia Press, 2000) was a finalist for the National Book Critics Circle Award in Criticism. Mr. Santos's awards include the Delmore Schwartz Memorial Award, the Discovery/The Nation Award, the Oscar Blumenthal Prize from *Poetry*, and an Academy Award from the American Academy of Arts and Letters. He has received fellowships from the Ingram Merrill and Guggenheim foundations, and the National Endowment for the Arts. He is a professor of English at the University of Missouri-Columbia.

JEFFREY SKINNER has published three volumes of poetry, including *Late Stars* (Wesleyan University Press); *A Guide to Forgetting* (Graywolf Press, winner in the National Poetry Series), and *The Company of Heaven* (Pitt Poetry Series, 1992). His work has garnered grants and fellowships from the National Endowment for the Arts, the Ingram Merrill Foundation, the Howard Foundation, Yaddo, McDowell, the Provincetown Arts Center, and three state arts agencies, among others. His poems have appeared in *The New Yorker, The Atlantic, Poetry, The Paris Review,* and *American Poetry Review*. His fourth book of poems, *The Moving Sidewalk*, will be published by Miami University Press. He is currently the Director of Creative Writing at the University of Louisville,

Kentucky, and editorial consultant for Sarabande Books. He lives in Louisville with his wife, the poet and publisher Sarah Gorham, and their two teenage daughters, Laura and Bonnie.

LUCI TAPAHONSO has written seven books of Native American poetry and stories, including *Songs of Shiprock Fair* (Kiva, 1999); *Blue Horses Rush In* (University of Arizona Press, 1997); *Navajo ABC: A Dineh Alphabet Book* (Macmillan, 1995); *Sáanii Dahataal: The Women Are Singing* (University of Arizona Press, 1993), which won a Southwest Book Award from the Border Regional Library Association; and *A Breeze Swept Through* (University of New Mexico Press, 1987). She has taught at several schools, including the University of New Mexico and the University of Kansas. She writes for academic and poetry journals as well as popular magazines, including *New Mexico Magazine* and the *Navajo Times*.

SUE ELLEN THOMPSON is a graduate of Middlebury College, Vermont, and the Bread Loaf School of English (M.A.). Her first book of poems, *This Body of Silk*, was awarded the 1986 Samuel French Morse Prize and was published by Northeastern University Press. A second volume, *The Wedding Boat*, was published in 1995 by Owl Creek Press in Seattle. Her most current work, *The Leaving: New and Selected Poems*, was published in November 2000 by Autumn House Press. Ms. Thompson was the 1982 National Arts Club Scholar in Poetry and the 1987 Robert Frost Fellow at the Bread Loaf Writers' Conference. She received an Individual Artist Grant from the state of Connecticut in 1994, which she used to support a monthlong writing retreat on Ocracoke Island, North Carolina. In 1997 she joined the faculty at the New England Young Writers' Conference at Bread Loaf, and in 1997 and 1999 she was invited to read her work at the Aran Islands Poetry Festival in Galway, Ireland. She lives in Mystic, Connecticut, where she works as a freelance writer and editor.

ROSANNA WARREN is Emma MacLachlan Metcalf Professor of the Humanities at Boston University. Her most recent books are *Suppliant Women*, a verse translation of Euripides' play, with Stephen Scully (Oxford University Press, 1995); and *Stained Glass*, poems (Norton, 1993). Her awards include the Witter Bynner Prize from the American Academy of Arts and Letters, a Lila Wallace-Readers' Digest Award, and the Lamont Poetry Prize from the Academy of American Poets. She has received fellowships from the Guggenheim Foundation and the ACLS. She is a fellow of the American Academy of Arts & Sciences.

# ACKNOWLEDGMENTS

Every effort has been made to trace the ownership of copyrighted material and to secure the necessary permission to reprint the selections in this book. In the event of questions about the use of any material, the publisher, while expressing regret for any inadvertent error, will be happy to make the correction in future printings. Thanks are due to the following for permission to reprint the material listed below:

Julie Agoos: "Delphinium," from the poem "Calendar Year"; "Lowell House, Taunton Hill"; and "Intensive," from the poem "Abandonment," are from *Calendar Year*, published by Sheep Meadow Press and reprinted with their permission, and the permission of the poet. "Portrait from Senlis" and "An Afternoon's Activity" were first published in *Above the Land* (Yale University Press, 1987) and are reprinted here with permission of the poet and of Yale University Press.

Sharon Bryan: The essay "The Sound of Poetry" is reprinted with permission of the author. "Big Sheep Knocks You About," "Abracadabra," "What I Want," "One Basket," "The Same River Twice," and "Bad News" are reprinted with permission of the poet.

Robert Cording: "Against Consolation" first appeared in *Kenyon Review*, "Self-Portrait" first appeared in *Poetry*, "Gratitude," first appeared in *The Paris Review*, "Between Worlds" first appeared in *Image*, and "Sam Cooke: *Touch the Hem of His Garment*" first appeared in *DoubleTake* (No. 14, 1999). All these and "White Mountains" are reprinted by permission of the poet.

Mark Cox: "Things My Grandfather Must Have Said" and "The Will" first appeared in *Smoulder*, published by David Godine. "Black Olives," "Grain," "Poem at Forty," "Pulsar," and "Sonata" appeared in *Thirty-Seven Years from the Stone*, published by University of Pittsburgh Press. The poems are reprinted by permission of David Godine, University of Pittsburgh Press, and the poet.

John Engels: "Landslide," "Ghosts," and "Wakeful at Midnight" first appeared in *Walking to Cootehill: New and Selected Poems, 1958–1992*, © 1993 by John Engels, Middlebury College/University Press of New England. These poems are reprinted with the permission of the poet and University Press of New England. "The Dead," "My Mother's Heritage," "Rising Stream," and "Poem for Your Birthday" are reprinted with permission of the poet.

Kathy Fagan: "To A Reader" first appeared in *The Antioch Review* (V56 #1, Winter 1998) and in 1999 was published with "Driving It," "Blue," and "MOVING & ST RAGE" in *MOVING & ST RAGE*, published by University of North Texas Press. These poems have been reprinted with permission of the poet and University of North Texas Press. "The Weather They Were Written In" first appeared in *Connecticut Review* (V19 #1, Spring 1997) and is reprinted with permission of the poet.

Robert Frost: "The Road Not Taken," "Birches," "An Old Man's Winter Night," "A Patch of Old Snow," "The Hill Wife," and " 'Out, Out—' " are from *The Poetry of Robert Frost*, edited by Edward Connery Lathem, Copyright 1944 by Robert Frost, © 1916, 1969 by Henry Holt and Company, LLC. Reprinted by permission of Henry Holt & Co., LLC.

Christopher Gilbert: "Tourist (Walking at The Robert Frost Place)," "A Sorrow Since Sitting Bull," "To Get to My Extreme," "Leaving the Loop," "A Metaphor for Something that Plays Us," and "The Plum" are reprinted with permission of the poet.

David Graham: "The Poet Grows Less & Less Postmodern as Summer Advances" first appeared in *The Laurel Review*. "Summons," which first appeared in *Famous Reporter*; "The Dogs in Dutch Paintings," which first appeared in *Poetry International*; "Honeymoon Island" and "Homage to Sadie Bosheers," which first appeared in *The Cortland Review*; and "Vietnam Memorial" have also appeared in the book *Stutter Monk*, published by Flume Press, 2000. Grateful acknowledgment is made to these previous publishers. "Eviction Elegy" is previously unpublished. All poems are reprinted by permission of the poet.

Donald Hall: Donald Hall has graciously written the introduction to this volume. We wish to acknowledge his steady and continued support of The Frost Place, his encouragement to younger poets, and a spirit of loving kindness which, over the years, has nurtured us all.

Mark Halliday: "Unconversation" and "Sourdough," were first published in *New Orleans Review*; "This Man" first appeared in *The Miscellany* at the University of

Tennessee/Chattanooga. These and "Schnetzer Day," "Franconia," and "Why Must We Write" are reprinted with permission of the poet.

Robert Hass: "At Squaw Valley" and "The Couple" are previously unpublished and are reprinted with permission of the poet.

Denis Johnson: "The Rockefeller Collection of Primitive Art" and "The Monk's Insomnia" are reprinted from *The Throne of the Third Heaven of the Nations Millennium General Assembly*, published by HarperCollins, who granted permission to reprint.

Cleopatra Mathis: "What to Tip the Boatman?" first appeared in *Ploughshares* (Fall/Winter 1999); "What Disappears" first appeared in *Louisiana Literature* (Fall 1999); "Solstice" first appeared in *Seneca Review* (Fall 1999). These and "Noon," "Search," "The Return," and "Under Moose Mountain" are reprinted with permission of the poet.

William Matthews: "On the Porch at the Frost Place," "Civilization and Its Discontents," and "Loyal" are from *Selected Poems and Translations, 1969–1991*, copyright © 1992 by William Matthews. "Inspiration" is from *After All: Last Poems*, copyright © 1998 by the Estate of William Matthews. "My Father's Body" and "The Rented House in Maine" are from *Time and Money: New Poems*, copyright © 1995 by William Matthews. All poems are reprinted with the permission of Houghton Mifflin Company.

Gary Miranda: "Like Snow," "Triptych," and "Listeners at the Breathing Place," from *Listeners at the Breathing Place*; and "Witnessing," from *Grace Period*, were published by Princeton University Press. "Third Elegy," from *Duino Elegies*, by Rainer Maria Rilke and translated by Gary Miranda, was published by Azul Books, 1996. The poems are reprinted with permission of the publishers.

Stanley Plumly: "Naps," "Piano," and "Strays" first appeared in *The Atlantic Monthly*; "November 11, 1942–November 12, 1997" first appeared in *Gettysburg Review*. They were published with "Reading with the Poets," "Sickle," and "Infidelity" by Ecco/HarperCollins in Spring 2000 under the title *Now That My Father Lies Down Beside Me* and are reprinted with permission of the poet.

Katha Pollitt: "Collectibles" first appeared in *The New Yorker* (V65 #18, 1989); "Dreaming About the Dead" first appeared in *The New Yorker* (V64

#33, 1988); "Mandarin Oranges" first appeared in *The New Yorker* (V63 #1, 1987); and "Playground," "Small Comfort," and "Lives of the Nineteenth-Century Poetesses" also first appeared in *The New Yorker*. "Mind-Body Problem" first appeared in *The Atlantic*. "Happiness Writes White" first appeared in *Grand Street* (V8#2, Winter 1989) and in *A Book of Women Poets from Antiquity to Now*, edited by Aliki and Will Barnstone, published by Schocken Books, 1992, and is reprinted by permission of Schocken Books. All poems by Katha Pollitt are reprinted with permission of the poet.

Pattiann Rogers: "The Hummingbird: A Seduction" and "The Significance of Location" were previously published in *Firekeeper*, by Milkweed Editions, 1994, whose editors have granted permission to reprint these poems. "Predestination" first appeared in *TriQuarterly* (#73, Fall 1988). "Abundance and Satisfaction" first appeared in *The Best American Poetry in 1966*, edited by Adrienne Rich and published by Scribner's with whose permission this poem is reprinted. "Elinor Frost's Marble-Topped Kneading Table" and "Rolling Naked in the Morning Dew" are reprinted with the poet's permission.

Mary Ruefle: "No Comparison," "The Tragic Drama of Joy," and "Among the Musk Ox People" first appeared in *Fence* (V2 #1, Spring 1999); "Furthurness" first appeared in *American Letters and Commentary*; and "Silk Land" first appeared in *Volt*. "10 April" first appeared in *Shenandoah* (V47 #4, Winter 1997). All of Mary Ruefle's poems, as well as the essay "Frost Day Remarks," are reprinted with her permission.

Mary Jo Salter: "The Seven Weepers" first appeared in *A Kiss in Space*, published by Knopf, who has granted permission to reprint the poem.

Sherod Santos: "The Conversation," "Dairy Cows at Crawford Farm," "A Valley in the Shadow of North Hollywood," and "Book of Blessings" are reprinted with permission of the poet.

Donald Sheehan: The introductions to each poet's work were transcribed from Don Sheehan's remarks preceding their readings at the Frost Place Festival of Poetry, held annually in early August. His wisdom and grace embody the spirit of The Frost Place and touch all those involved in it, allowing many seeds planted there to bear fruit.

Jeffrey Skinner: "The Inadequacy," "The New Music Concert: A Drinking Dream" and "Closed Heads Wounds" first appeared in *American Poetry Review*. All of Jeffrey Skinner's poems are reprinted with permission of the poet.

Luci Tapahonso: "A Whispered Chant of Loneliness" is reprinted from *Sáanii Dahataal: The Women Are Singing* and is reprinted with permission of University of Arizona Press.

Sue Ellen Thompson: "Living at the Frost Place," "Echo Rock Farm," "After the Accident," "Fin de Siècle," "Parted," "The Mother's Dream," "The Empty Room," and "The Leaving" are reprinted with permission of the poet, and will appear in the poet's latest book, *The Leaving*, published by Autumn House Press.

Rosanna Warren: "The Cost" was first published in *The New Republic* (V199 #18, 1988). "Umbilical" first appeared in *Boulevard/92* of Drexel University. "Song" was published in *Poems for a Small Planet*, edited by Robert Pack and Jay Parini and is reprinted with additional permission of University Press of New England. These and "Mountain View," "The Twelfth Day," and "Season Due" were published in Ms. Warren's book *Stained Glass* (Norton, 1993) and are reprinted with permission of the poet.

# PHOTO CREDITS

## PHOTOS OF POETS

Star Black, pages 230, 340; Francois Camoin, page 354;
Patty Cassidy, page 70; Karen Durlach, page 154;
Brad Leithauser, page 98; William Matthews, Sr., page 84;
John McIver, pages 48, 184, 292, 326;
Vincent McGroary, pages 104, 120, 128, 140, 168, 200, 214, 246, 262;
Jill Rosser, page 278; Lee Shippey, page 298;
Robert Selden Smith, page 62

## OTHER PHOTOS

All photos by Star Black
except
frontispiece by Ken Heyman

pages 17, 24, 199, 353 by Bruce Richards